MASS MEDIA

Those of us with an interest in social problems can scarcely afford
to ignore the importance of the media in the contemporary world.
In most people's timetables the number of hours spent reading
papers, watching TV or listening to the radio comes third, after
sleep and work. The media are a major source of information,
of entertainment and, because of advertising, a major factor in
economic development. Outstanding books have been written on
film, television and newspapers, but the interaction between these
media, their relation to each other and to society as a whole are
generally ignored. This book attempts to take into account the
whole 'system' of information and entertainment and to define,
on the basis of the present state of theory and with reference to
a number of case studies, the conditions and prerequisites for a
wide-ranging enquiry into the media and their different uses in
societies. The author examines how audiences develop, evaluates
tastes and analyses some of the major technical changes which
have occurred in the last century. He considers the role of the
media in entertainment and information. Finally he explores
how media empires evolve.

Lively and accessible, this book will appeal to students of
sociology, cultural studies and communication studies.

Pierre Sorlin is Professor of Sociology of Audio-Visual Communication at the University of Paris III.

KEY IDEAS
Series Editor: Peter Hamilton
The Open University

KEY IDEAS
Series Editor: PETER HAMILTON
The Open University, Milton Keynes

Designed to complement the successful *Key Sociologists*, this series covers the main concepts, issues, debates, and controversies in sociology and the social sciences. The series aims to provide authoritative essays on central topics of social science, such as community, power, work, sexuality, inequality, benefits and ideology, class, family, etc. Books adopt a strong individual 'line' constituting original essays rather than literary surveys, and form lively and original treatments of their subject matter. The books will be useful to students and teachers of sociology, political science, economics, psychology, philosophy, and geography.

THE SYMBOLIC CONSTRUCTION OF COMMUNITY
ANTHONY P. COHEN, Department of Social Anthropology, University of Manchester
SOCIETY
DAVID FRISBY and DEREK SAYER, Department of Sociology, University of Manchester
SEXUALITY
JEFFREY WEEKS, Social Work Studies Department, University of Southampton
WORKING
GRAEME SALAMAN, Faculty of Social Sciences, The Open University, Milton Keynes
BELIEFS AND IDEOLOGY
KENNETH THOMPSON, Faculty of Social Sciences, The Open University, Milton Keynes
EQUALITY
BRYAN TURNER, School of Social Sciences, The Flinders University of South Australia
HEGEMONY
ROBERT BOCOCK, Faculty of Social Sciences, The Open University, Milton Keynes
RACISM
ROBERT MILES, Department of Sociology, University of Glasgow
POSTMODERNITY
BARRY SMART, Associate Professor of Sociology, University of Auckland, New Zealand
CLASS
STEPHEN EDGELL, School of Social Sciences, University of Salford

MASS MEDIA

PIERRE SORLIN

London and New York

Coventry University

PO4790

First published 1994
by Routledge
11 New Fetter Lane London EC4P 4EE

Simultaneously published in the USA and Canada
by Routledge
29 West 35th Street, New York NY 10001

© 1994 Pierre Sorlin

Typeset in Times by Intype, London

Printed and bound in Great Britain by
Clays Ltd, St Ives PLC

British Library Cataloguing in Publication Data

A catalogue record for this book is available from the British Library.

Library of Congress Cataloging in Publication Data has been applied for

ISBN 0–415–11023–8 ISBN 0–415–07209–3 (pbk)

Contents

Acknowledgements

Many people have contributed, directly or indirectly, to the elaboration of this book. I owe a debt to Peter Hamilton who fathered the first idea of the work and then stimulated my research. While I was writing, I had long, often controversial talks with David Buxton, Danny Dayan and Paddy Scannell, whose influence can be detected in many pages. I am most grateful to the graduate students of the Sorbonne who forced me to elucidate my views and make them more explicit.

Introduction

Imagine a newcomer has entered your room. It is not a human being, only a book. But just as people need to be introduced, so do books. If we want to make use of them, we need to know their aims and purposes.

The title of this volume speaks for itself. We have all heard of those means of communication, namely the press, television, radio, cinema and posters, which convey information and purvey entertainment throughout the world. I am not attempting to describe them here, for my readers know very well what they are. I am more interested in understanding how we experience the media. On the one hand, they are 'real' objects, as palpable as pieces of furniture; on the other hand, they draw us into a world taken for granted, although what is said or shown does not happen in front of us. My concern is with this duality and the workings of our daily routines: what part do the media play in our lives? How do we accept, or reject what they tell us? How far do they try to sway our thinking? This is a critical essay aimed at questioning its readers' practices.

Masses and media

To begin with, are we bound to consider the two nouns, 'mass' and 'media', as given? Even if the compound expression is familiar to us, its components have been insufficiently considered. What constitutes 'mass'? What do we mean by 'media'? It is true that short words are very convenient and it is reasonable to prefer the term 'mass media' to the phrase 'influential and widely diffused means of communication'. However, this does not account for the choice of the two terms which, taken together, give 'mass media' its verbal form and meaning.

A mass is a lump of matter; the word itself conveys a notion of weight and quantity. Military observers signal when a general has 'massed' his troops for an attack indicating a serious threat for the other side. And, for many of us, the most salient feature of modern industry is mass production, which means cheap and short-lived items desired by the multitudes. I do not need to point out that the word 'mass' has come to have strong negative connotations, linked as it often is to other terms to which it adds a depreciative nuance. 'Mass art' (e.g. industrialized furniture, comic-strips, pop music) attempts to please the majority and ignores the refinement of 'pure' art. Mass culture is sold at bargain prices. Mass-circulation magazines are filled with gossip and the nadir is probably reached when objects are aimed at the housewife.

In its more practical sense, related to weight, the word mass has been in the language for many centuries but used in its current sense it is rather recent. Until late in the nineteenth century, the prevalent word for evoking fear and suspicion was 'multitude' and, during the French Revolution, 'mob' was a very evocative word to characterize an unsteady, easy to mobilize crowd. But why did the word 'mass' prevail over 'mob'? Some historians would say that the ruling class, having witnessed migrations from rural areas to the cities and industrialization, believed that it would soon itself be merged into 'the mass' of uneducated, unskilled people. However, I think that such 'realistic' explanations miss the point. There was after all no precise reason for politicians and moralists to denounce the vulgarity and tastelessness of the 'masses' but, once they had begun to do so, it became increasingly 'obvious' that there was something untoward about the masses.

What concerns us more than etymology and early usage is

the fact that the word, like any endlessly repeated term, has created a conviction. The 'adoption' of an expression follows a classic process. After a while it assumes a life of its own and emerges as an indisputable fact in speeches, newspapers and even in the discourse of universities. The idea of 'mass' has numbed our powers of observation. We believe we are in a mass society because the word 'mass' has become associated with the most obvious aspects of our current universe. But, instead of being merely a tool which can help us describe what we observe, it is presumed to be a fact. It is a preconception which prevents proper thinking: if we have indeed entered the age of the masses, we must find facts which square with the metaphor.

Originally, a medium is something lying in a middle or inter-mediate position – an agent, an object through which a purpose is accomplished. In other words there are two poles (for instance, two people) and between them a medium (for instance, a tele-phone or a fax). Nowadays, the media are the means by which information or entertainment are diffused. Who are they linking to whom? Again, we are trapped by words. Whenever there is a medium, there is necessarily someone who acts and someone who receives and we cannot refrain from referring to the image conveyed by the term 'medium' which means 'something between'. It was partially to counteract this stereotype that Mar-shall McLuhan launched his famous paradox: 'the medium is the message'. What he wanted to clarify was that any medium, because it is an instrument, modifies our hold over the world and consequently our interpretation of experience. We make sense of the universe in different ways depending on whether we look around us, read newspapers or watch television.[1] McLuhan's assumption is, to a certain extent, commonplace; two people behave differently depending on whether they talk by phone or send faxes to one another. It is helpful, however, to emphasize the fact that what is known as 'the media' includes a large variety of components and that study of the media must not follow the oversimplified scheme: sender/medium/destination.

An awkward expression

The expression 'mass media' is a strange, awkward one, it has given rise to countless clichés in relation to the masses and the function of the media, but it does not pinpoint any specific set of objects or practices. Sociology is often confronted with preformed schemes which are interesting and deserve close scrutiny, not because they throw light on problems of our time but because they belong to a group's or to 'society's' shared group of conceptions. Specialists disagree on the definition of 'mass media'; they are at odds on various points, because their starting points are different. We do not want to pass judgement, but think it more important to understand how this new expression was coined and circulated. Why is it that systems as different as posters and radio, newspapers and films have come to seem like the basic elements of a unique whole? There are, of course, many possible answers to the question and those that I am going to stress are not necessarily the most important ones but those most likely to help us understand how the fiction of the term 'mass media' has been contrived.

Unlike other media, cinema succeeded very quickly. It won an audience within about a decade and it provides us with an example of peoples' response to a new form of entertainment and information. There were heated debates over cinema at the beginning of the twentieth century, many opinion leaders denouncing films as a form of barbarism which would destroy the legacy of the past. We shall come back to these points of discussion later and we shall see that both popular newspapers and television were cursed in a similar manner over a much longer period. The point here is that the status of respectability was accorded to a few films because they reached the standards demanded in the already legitimate arts, namely literature, drama and painting, whereas the standard film was considered to be uninspiring or even dangerous. Questions of aesthetic differences or of the relative qualities of one practice as compared with another were not discussed. Cinema was accepted, when it was accepted at all, not because it was original, unpredictable and vigorous but because it resembled theatre. All the media have in common the fact that many educated people view them as uninteresting and as having a tendency to corrupt.

We must not be too dismissive of those who condemned cinema, the press or television, because they were aware of a highly relevant aspect, namely their close association with commerce. Items intended for wide consumption are not made in conditions to favour individual artistic expression; they are intended to make profits. Artists, of course, always need money but they also work with the future in mind, whereas business tycoons are primarily concerned with benefiting themselves and not with publishing books or making films which will still be famous a century hence. The media prosper on the churning-out of short-lived products and in this respect they are typical of the industrial era. It is not particularly illuminating to pinpoint when an expression was 'first' used because such an expression is generally accepted only after it has circulated, more or less unnoticed, for a long time. Nevertheless, it seems that the term 'mass media' was introduced by advertising companies anxious to persuade their clients that publicity in the media would greatly increase the number of customers.

Inasmuch as they inform, the media are part of the communication process, that is to say they are part of the special and unique process by which human communities are formed and in which they live. Mankind uses many devices to communicate and verbal language must be thought of only as the most convenient instrument to deliver long, complex messages. However, it is still true that linguistic communication has generally been given greater attention than other forms of communication because we are enabled to think clearly once we have mastered a language. One of the reasons why all the media were at first included in the same conceptual entity was that, for some time, because they were used to deliver messages, they were all treated as various aspects of the written or spoken language.

There was confusion over the matter, but there was more to it than that. Linguistics, the study of verbal language, has been developing so quickly and efficiently since the end of the nineteenth century that it has often been taken as a model theory, capable of accounting for all the things we can express and understand. What is unfortunate with such a generalization is not only that a theory (or rather theories) elaborated for a particular language has been extended to other forms of expression, it is also that the patterns by which a language functions have been applied to other, basically different cases. A correct understanding of a verbal expression is to be derived from the accuracy of its arrangement; for example, in formal terms, 'drink Englishmen beer' is meaningless. It is thus tempting to define the simpler parts of non-verbal 'languages' (the equivalent to words) and then to evaluate the meaning of the so-called 'sentences' used in posters or films.

However, if the notion of correction is central to any theory of understanding, it is not sufficient. It must be supplemented by an analysis of the conditions in which the utterance is being made. For instance, we can only make sense of the utterance 'drink Englishmen beer' if we know that the person addressing us does not speak English well. What is crucial is not deciphering the message, but our thoughts and feelings for, and our knowledge of, the sender. Direct application of linguistics to non-verbal expressions is inadequate. However, it is only when it became clear that most media give rise to texts which cannot be adequately reproduced on paper (and, what is more, that electronic information, being formally different from written information, is not merely an electronic shadow of the printed page), that new questions emerged.

Economic factors, the prejudices of those in a position to express an opinion and the dominance of a linguistic method of investigation have all contributed in conferring on the mass media their seeming cohesion. It would not be arduous to find other explanations but we're not trying to account for the haphazard gathering together of fairly different media. We are content to stress the fact that a variety of 'causes' converged to create a supposed entity, the existence of which few people would question today.

The temptation of history

No sociologist would consider a universally accepted category such as 'mass media' to be self-explanatory and indisputable. And very few of them confronted by an impossibly large amount of empirical data would start fact-collecting in the hope that, by listing and ordering such facts they could produce a synthetic representation of any value. Essentially, the sociologist's task is to produce theoretical instruments capable of critically evaluating the immense diversity of social phenomena. In order to deduce conclusions from the available material, such theoretical instruments must be based on simple, unambiguous principles. But, in pursuing these aims the sociologist is exposed to three main temptations, namely those presented by functional analysis, history and reverence towards established theories.

Functional analysis by its very nature presents a picture of homogeneity and continuity. Too many studies which employ it consist merely of sketches concerning the 'specificity' of the various media, the manner of their production and distribution and assumptions regarding their influence. Descriptive activities are far from useless; they provide their readers, whether sociologists or lay people, with as much information as possible and help to clarify the various problems in the field. Unless we think of the media as pre-existent,[2] we shall find we have problems even in determining what to focus on. Should we speak of 'television' as a universal entity, or the various television networks, or the different channels? Should we speak of what we have seen on a given day – or of programmes which run daily for years? Should we speak of a series, or of the contribution of an individual on a precise day? In other words, how can we say universally valid things about practices which show no tendency to uniformity and which are characterized by constant diversification and evolution rather than by continuity? How is it possible to sustain the notion of the scientific authority of sociology while having so little hope that the application of vague, ill-defined notions such as 'the media' or 'the masses' will be ultimately validated by social evolution itself?

Hence, the interest and value of a historical approach based on the acceptance of change and pluralism. We cannot ignore the progress of technology and that most new techniques take up where the last left off. Is there any connection between the relative determinism inherent in technological dynamism and the manner in which people are informed, the manner in which they experience and interpret the world in which they live? This is a crucial issue that we shall discuss at length. While it is not our aim to produce a history of communications, we shall not forget the innumerable liaisons and circularities between technological change and its cultural materialization in the context of engineering innovation, government regulations and profit making. History will help us, but only as a subordinate partner. Historians believe that we must place cultural productions, such as the media, within the social, economic and political context of their time, in order to reveal how they served the power of class or sectional interests. But to approach our subject in this way, necessarily, we lose sight of a medium's capacity to address different publics in different ways. It means we distance ourselves from the media as if we were not enclosed within their universe.

This, of course, raises the related issue of what value historians suppose their own interpretations to serve. However, it is up to them to decide whether their research can be effective without a system of references (e.g. a theoretical framework) stable enough to preserve them from subjectivism. But, without being professional historians ourselves, we are also concerned by the range of effects which historical curiosity has brought to bear on the universe of the media; history is not only a representation of the past delineated by specialists but also part of peoples' daily lives. The media, and especially radio and television, which continually recall what they were like ten, twenty or more years ago, have become the self-defining subjects of their own historical transformations. Their programmes do not simply mirror the past, but contribute to its reactivation, even to its creation; an image of an event does not necessarily immediately follow its occurrence, it may be 'frozen' and resurface much later. The production of history, instead of being an objective assessment of past events, has become part of the media.

One therefore suspects that because of the variety of particular events which could be taken into account and because of the virtual infinity of possible combinations and relationships between them, history, which is effective in ordering and reordering the data it has collected, is unable to propound a coherent, synthetic approach to the media.

Theories, yesterday and today

Unlike historians, sociologists are not content to simply observe phenomena; they want to manipulate their 'universe' – the field they try to plough – by performing experiments on it; they need to test the range of data for which they have to account, and to know to what extent they can make predictions. To put it differently, sociologists must have recourse to a theory, or rather to a theoretical framework, by means of which observed phenomena can be interpreted. The trouble is that there are no rules for finding the right analogy on which the formulation of such theories depends. There is no logical reason to endorse theories which are more or less elegant, simple and all-encompassing but which are only temporary, highly arguable implements.

Throughout the twentieth century, Marxism has been one of the most often referred to and most seductive theories as far as the media are concerned. Its attraction lies in the fact that it provides an explanation of what the media are, and what their social function is. In *The German Ideology*, Marx sees all those who are dominated as accepting their ideas from the ruling class because it is this class which controls the means of mental production. This is not just a question of propaganda: problems are always presented from the point of view of and with the concepts of the rulers. Ideology comprises the cluster of meanings, institutions and practices which furnish the framework within which people organize their actions so that even those who protest and criticize use ideological tools created by their enemies. But is this sufficient to account for the fact that power is seldom seriously threatened by those subject to it? Probably not. News is not only diffused by the media but also has a symbolic value, which helps people to classify themselves in relation to others (Am I mentioned in the newspaper? Who is mentioned with me, and who has been omitted?). Gramsci therefore refined Marx's initial formulation by introducing the notion of 'consensus' which attempted to explain why people abide by the rules of the dominant class even when they are not constrained by force. In most cases, even in dictatorships, power relations have been shaped not just by recourse to terror but also by acceptance. When reading the newspapers, or watching television we enclose ourselves in a circle of unwitting complicity with our leaders; we accept the value of what those men say or do. This is not an independent resource used by the powerful in order to get their ideas accepted by the powerless; people conceive of their life as 'normal' because it is their daily life and they forget that it has been imposed upon them by the most powerful.

Ideology and consensus are not objects which can be tested; they are merely assumptions which may help us account for the existence or absence of unrest. What do they consist of? The thing that makes these notions slightly pernicious is that while they look very useful they are in fact difficult to deal with. For instance, how can we assess the existence and extent of consensus in a given society? Since it cannot be measured, it is always tempting to equate consensus with the manipulation of public opinion and to evaluate the degree of acceptance by studying the messages diffused by the media, regardless of their practical impact. If the ideas of ideology and consent are to be maintained, they must not be confused with what is said in the media.

Marxists oppose the bourgeoisie and the proletariat, exploiters and exploited, etc. In doing so, they generate dichotomies and work on structures. If Marxism, as a theory, has been especially influential for the study of the media, structuralism was the most respected method during the second third of this century. Marxism states that human evolution has been orientated by class struggle. It is a large, all-encompassing theory which provides a 'key' to interpret history. Structuralism, however, claims to be no more than a systematic way of solving problems. Contrary to what has often been stated, structuralists do not believe that anything can be understood by means of simple opposites such as cooked/raw or nature/nurture; they merely think that the significant features of a given thing are better defined by looking at the features of its opposite. This is widely true for simple phenomena but does not apply to complicated matters. It is true that an initial approach to the media can be organized around the opposition existing between those who own them and those who passively consume them. However, this division does not tell us very much. Changes and tendencies which cannot be accounted for by the notion of possession/lack of possession affect the making of information. The media therefore have to be seen in relation to such processes as the rise of the metropolis or the development of international trade, and to such institutions as the law, religion and the state.

It could be argued that structuralism was something readily understood by social scientists at a time when the world was divided between two superpowers. The end of the Cold War, coupled with the sudden collapse in the political credibility and, more simply, the very existence of communism meant that no general theory such as Marxism, no simple method like structuralism could link a vast array of disciplines united, hopefully at any rate, by the conviction that there was one correct procedure and one final explanation. The re-evaluation that comes at the end of any critical period does not necessarily entail a total rejection of the previously accepted method and theory. Marxism still has something to tell us about the logic of capitalism and structuralism helps us to define things by observing contrasts between them. What has changed is that, between two terms employing opposition, scientists now often find a third possibility. While accepting that the couple black/white works well in some circumstances, they now perceive there are cases in which the whole spectrum which goes from one extreme to the other must be taken into account.

In the last decades of this century, the social sciences have entered the age of postmodernism or rather of deconstructionism. This new trend must not be considered a total break with social criticism as previously developed. Deconstructionism, while dealing seriously with the structures of social and cultural authority, and while challenging the liberal humanist ideology, considers any topic too large for anyone to think about as a whole, the only recourse being thus to approach it piecemeal, to merely consider bits of it. It argues that any event is irreducible to an atemporal meaning, that we cannot classify human behaviour since the complexities inherent in it lose their specificity once they are confined within a conceptual identity such as class conflict or rivalry between generations.

Deconstructionism must not, however, be confused with relativism which holds that 'truth' is not absolute but changes with time and location. Deconstructionists argue that a claim does not necessitate a claim incongruent with it being considered 'false'. Accepting that the limitations of the human horizon prohibit the formulation of any universally valid statement, they stress the fact that we cannot distinguish between the constructed nature of our perception and the 'independent' structure of the world. Modernism, they claim, was an attempt to define modern society in clear-cut terms. This gave it a fallacious coherence since the various aspects of society were made to fit together only at the expense of simplifying what they were in themselves. Deconstructionism ceases to use 'society' as a general noun having a general meaning and refuses to speak of 'history' as a revelation of how 'society' is created in time. While previous theories aimed at unifying the processes they observed, Deconstructionism considers significant and worthy of interest both discontinuity and fragmentation. It is prepared to explore improvisation, sudden changes of policy or orientation or, to stay in our field of research, the patchwork composition of human groups such as 'those who have bought the *Sun* today'.

Theories stand above, or outside social practices and attempt to account for them. Deconstructionism is not alien to practices, it accords priority to them and accepts them for what they are. It is not therefore a theory: only a state of mind, an intention which prevents us from believing that the media, or producers, or audiences are anything other than labels which can be useful but which do not exist outside the field in which and for which they have been contrived. At the same time, deconstructionism urges us to adopt a phenomenological approach to the problems we want to study by focusing on the actions and consciousness of people instead of concentrating on social structures since it is no longer possible that identity can be inferred from our place in the social structure.

To be more specific, social research has for several years been emphasizing the role of agents, editors, publishers and readers in providing the media with their meaning. One of the key features of this new approach to the media is the active and enhanced responsibility it places on the user. Every text is designed in such a way that it has one order but simultaneous recourse to different texts, for instance to television and newspapers, creates different orders and calls for commitment from the user in devising an appropriate, personal method of reading. Not only do readers explore different texts and at different levels, but, for them, such texts are linked by a multiplicity of routes and are explored in a large variety of ways.

So we may now ask whether, under the impact of deconstructionism, it is still possible to define a sociological project. The founders of sociology stressed the universality of their science in contrast with the particularism of other research in the humanities but we are no longer able to entirely agree with them. The world as mapped by contemporary researchers looks very different from that explored by their predecessors about a century ago. The human sphere, today, has a chaotic appearance and we must accept that sociology is unable to champion general theories. What is generally known as the 'mass media' also presents a chaotic appearance and is of paramount interest in this respect. We cannot define what we mean by the term but many people think they know what constitutes the mass media and that it plays a fundamental part in our awareness of the world. It derives its apparent reality from the widely shared assumption that it does in fact exist. Our task is therefore to question the relationship of readers, or viewers (who may have only a simple idea of what they understand by 'mass media'), with the media with which they interact daily. Certainly ours is an inquiry which lacks the profundity of one underlined by an all-encompassing theory founded on 'certainty' of one sort or another. Nevertheless, ours will have more variety and is likely to produce conflicting material indicative of the vast and changing function of media in the present-day world.

Chapter 1 starts with various definitions of a 'public' put forward by representatives of the media themselves and also by social scientists. It goes on to consider the formation of audiences. Chapter 2 deals with the expectations of the users and evaluates how they make sense of what they are offered by the media. Chapter 3 explores how media empires are built and evolve in the contemporary world. It may seem strange to start with as imprecise a notion as that of 'audience' and to end with the study of big corporations which represent the most obvious aspect of the mass media. This has been done intentionally: we consider it better to start with more arguable matters and then, once the reader has accepted the very facts of diversity and incertitude, to introduce elements of certainty.

NOTES

1 M. McLuhan, *Understanding Media* (1964, New York, McGraw Hill), p. 32ff.
2 It is not because newspapers or films are available that scientists are interested in media; the notion and study of mass media are partially independent from the circulation of media; this point will be developed in Chapter 1; see especially note 3.

1
Audiences

Sceptics sometimes wonder whether sociology can teach us anything that other disciplines, anthropology, or psychology, or political sciences do not already know; the answer is that sociology alone tries to understand why human beings, unlike most living beings, cannot live but in permanent interaction with one another. Sociologists have always been anxious to illuminate the kinds of links which exist inside mankind and their postulates, contradictory though they are, will help us to see how the relationships between the media and those who practise them influence social cohesion.

Durkheim distinguished two sorts of cohesion characteristic, respectively, of 'traditional' and 'industrial' societies. Of course, these types are pure artefacts. We must not believe that they have ever been realized. We are even obliged to recognize that Durkheim's model is a typical, almost caricatured example of structural partition. Let us see what it may still tell us. According to Durkheim, the members of less-advanced societies share the same beliefs and perform the same rituals.[1] As we shall see, the practice of media use is highly ritualized. Our buying of 'our' papers is perfectly routinized and we are aware of the fact that, every night, about ten million listeners switch on their television set for the *Nine O'clock News*.

We shall also see that the media create myths, not because of what they 'say' but because they offer us patterns to observe our universe by contrasting, for instance, politics and short news items. The expectations of the reader/listener, renewed day after day, create the dimensions of an unwitting, purely 'mechanical' to borrow Durkheim's expression – type of 'solidarity', although the texts or programmes which are being diffused do not call for cohesion. What counts is not the impact on their minds of what readers/listeners learn (for this will usually remain unverifiable, especially since what is told by media is often a matter of opinion, not of 'pure' fact) but rather the force of repetition it carries. Durkheim was aware of the existence of 'mechanical' solidarities in industrial, more advanced societies, but he saw them as a persistence of older beliefs. It is therefore interesting to point out that, besides rituals inherited from the past, new rituals, rituals born from industrialization itself (for instance the industrial production and distribution of papers or broadcast information), can appear in a modern society.

What makes one feel uncomfortable about Durkheim's division is its strictness: *this* or *that* (even if *that* encroaches upon *this*). Weber's model which contrasts sociation and communality[2] looks as rigid but Weber is intent on explaining that these are only two opposed poles and that there is a wide range of actual combinations between them. In a sociation, people gather for a precise task; they may differ, and even be hostile, about everything, but their common aim reunites them, at least temporarily. New media, in the earliest phases of their development, have generally created sociations; in the first half of the nineteenth century, neighbours or friends joined to subscribe to a paper which was much too expensive for any of them; today, in underdeveloped countries, a radio or a television set is often owned collectively. We shall enlarge later upon this extremely important question. Suffice to note, for the time being, that media are likely to create a passing solidarity between otherwise indifferent people. Communality, in Weber's view, is not as precisely defined as sociation. It exists when people have something in common – ideas, beliefs or even kinship. Unlike sociation, communality may be deprived of any material organization. How can we, then, decide that there is a community? By evaluating the chances that, given their state of mind, people will perform a certain type of

action or conform to a certain behaviour. Do you avoid calling
your friends during television's 'prime time'? If you do, your
motivation is that your friends might be disturbed. Your compliance with the television time table, your behaviour, adapted to
that of the others, show that you are a member of the communality of the 'prime-timers'.

We do not want to carry on with Durkheim or Weber's categories. These were coined in a universe different from ours where
newspapers, advertisements and even cinema were already of paramount importance, but were not given the dignity of 'media'.
Weber, who scrutinized carefully the nature of power and the functions of political parties in *Economy and Society*, did not speak of
the press in his book and yet, at the time he was writing it
(1911–1913), the circulation of dailies, in Germany, was larger than
today and all political groupings had their own press. Practical
activities and concepts do not develop at the same pace and the
notion of media began to be used well after the launching of most
media.[3] This does not mean that we do not care about the evolution
of the different means of communication: many changes cannot be
fully understood without a minimal knowledge of what happened
previously. It is even necessary, in some aspects, to go as far back as
the early seventeenth century. If the intellectual framework in
which Durkheim or Weber conceived of social exchange is inadequate for our research because it does not allow us to raise the
question we would like to explore, it is still worth noticing that their
models force us to take into account the variety of connections
involved in the practice of the media.

There is no immunity against the media. Even people who
never read a newspaper and have no television set are surrounded
by messages, be it only advertisements stuck on walls, which they
cannot ignore. With the whole world being thus a latent public,
it is vital for the companies which run magazines or television
networks to know how many customers they can reach. Hence,
the fortune of specialized organizations which 'measure' the size
of actual or potential audiences; measurement attains an impressive degree of sophistication. The system called *Computerized
Continuous Preference Indication* is said to check the behaviour
of all the members of a panel and even to test the depth of their
participation. Firms have collected a vast amount of data that
social scientists might use to evaluate the comportment, inclinations and options of readers or viewers. 'Meaning', that is to say
the content of papers or broadcast programmes, is not necessarily

involved in this process; we shall try, later, to work out why messages emitted by the media make sense for those who get them, but what we would like to examine, first, is another, much simpler thing: media sell goods (their messages) that people buy directly (a paper, a seat in a cinema) or indirectly (a broadcast programme): how is it possible to account for the various attitudes of the consumers? Journalists are often criticized for delivering false or exaggerated news but we must not forget that they work under the pressure of a permanent demand; the desire for media is relatively stable, it cannot be simply equated with a hunt for information or entertainment. Statistical surveys seem to provide us with exceptionally good material, but we have to verify whether it fits in with our research.[4] And if it does not, even partially, we must find out how audiences can be best described.

THE MEDIA AND 'THEIR' PUBLIC

From people to public

Media are directed towards an anonymous entity, the public. David Chaney considers the notion of 'public' to be an example of a fiction,[5] which does not mean that it is a pure fantasy but that it is mostly characterized by its narrative construction. When we say that the public is the set of people who get their information and opinion from mass media, we set up a fictitious entity, a collective person who buys newspapers or switches on the television, receives news and assimilates it; the narrative sequence explains very well how the readers/listeners get the messages and are influenced by them, but we are not allowed to assert that this very simple process is the dominant one. Things might be rather different if we did not take for granted the inescapable succession of stages such as desire, fulfilment and acceptance. We shall therefore open this chapter by questioning the very notion of public.

The term 'public' itself is a strange word which can be traced back to the sixteenth century; it sounds more or less alike in most Indo-European languages and its spelling has not changed since it was first found in texts. It is a 'fossilized' word all the more open to various interpretations since its form is immutable. It derives from the Latin *populus* which has also given rise to 'people' (something that the Spanish understand very well for the Spanish word for 'people' is *pueblo*). The word 'public' begins to be widely used in the eighteenth century and it means 'the people' as opposed to aristocracy. Politics, it was assumed at the time, should no longer be the exclusive concern of a minority, it should be 'publicized' and discussed publicly. The sphere of public life has long been an open space. It has developed in meetings, conversations in the street and debates in pubs. Yet, significantly the word 'public' tends more and more to refer to an unorganized, amorphous body which is merely a nominal plural.

How can we account for that shift in meaning? A possible answer can be found in the development of cheap, easily accessible means of information at the end of the nineteenth century. Significantly, the *Daily Mail*, the paper with the biggest circulation at the start of the twentieth century, was launched in 1896, the year in which the cinema became a public entertainment. In the same period, education improved dramatically. A huge literate public previously deprived of tradition came into being and it was to cater for this that the popular newspapers were published and films were made. Mass production implied the division of labour in 'public' activities. Up until the middle of the nineteenth century almost everyone could print and circulate hastily made leaflets, whereas since then, the press has become an expensive, highly specialized business. By making sales figures their only preoccupation, the press barons modified the function of papers. They provided their reader with private news and trivial events which, unlike political (= public) facts, could not give way to arguments, thus destroying the close interdependence between the journalists and their customers and transforming an active public into a group of news consumers.

Later, we shall try to determine whether the changes which occurred at the outset of the present century were as radical as is often said. Let us acknowledge, for the moment, that the theories we have just mentioned are important because they stress extremely important modifications. In doing so, they do not explain why a given word has taken on another meaning. David Chaney is perfectly correct when he calls the 'public' a fiction. It is too vague a term and tends to unify a huge variety of behaviours behind a common label. Why do media, instead of speaking of an abstract entity, not talk of their patrons, that is to say, of fairly different people? The fiction is widely accepted, even by those who study the politics of information, and we must therefore understand why it is so convenient: determining how the media imagine their public to be is a preliminary step to our enquiry.

Measuring audiences

Publishers have always noted how many of their books they could sell. Theatre directors have anxiously controlled, night after night, the variations in the size of their audiences. But the notion that what was so carefully observed could be defined as 'our public' came late, when the Treasury, or other financial institutions, were interested in checking how much money had been collected. The best, most reliable figures have been arranged for taxation. The British statistics for television have been exceptionally precise since the 1950s, not because the British are more mathematically oriented than other people but because the licence fee is particularly high in the United Kingdom and because advertisement was authorized earlier here than in most other countries. Sociologists know that fiscal documents have something to tell us about taxation rules, sometimes about the revenue from tax, but do not reflect actual practices, since many people, willingly or not, escape the law. An amusing example concerns French radio; up until 1935, there was a steady increase in the acquisition of radio sets in France but, in 1936, the number fell heavily. It might be tempting to infer from statistics that, the year the Popular Front came to power, France was losing her interest in politics, but there is a much simpler explanation: notably, the licence fee was raised at the beginning of 1936 and many buyers did not give their name; as a result we have no way of correlating the number of potential listeners with the events which stood out in that year.

Statistics, which are first and foremost collections of numbers, are sometimes seen as explanatory since they enable certain phenomena to be understood in the form of simple, indisputable data. All too often, audience surveys infer decisive changes from personal tastes or empirical observations and fail to place individuals in the social settings in which choices are made. To say that the *Sun* increased its sales after it had been transformed into a tabloid newspaper is an imprecise, arguable statement, whereas to observe that sales jumped from one to three million copies within two years (1970–72) is evaluative and more conclusive. If we go as far as comparing figures relating to different tabloids, we may detect recurrences which reveal habits and then establish a series which could be an explanation for why the newspaper sales increased in Britain, in the 1970s. Statistics which seem to speak for themselves (a trebling is an impressive result) have gradually

come to be seen not as useful tools but as facts, as real phenomena which can account for other phenomena. It is tempting to
bypass challenging questions by resorting to statistical evidence;
peaks in sales can be read as a triumph in reader interest, the
number and length of quotations in other media is easily interpreted as favourable reception and if these two series coincide,
who would deny that a newspaper has won a popular audience?
In fact, we are not allowed to take sales figures as the basis for
inferences about popularity. The only possible conclusion is that
the clientele has increased but we don't know whether or not
they read a newspaper or watch television attentively. There may
be more readers or viewers and a lower level of attention. What
is more, changes in attitude towards the media are often erratic so
that in attributing some significance to an impressive but specific
infatuation we are in danger of overrating the importance of
statistics and mistaking a passing fancy for a revolution.

The issue at stake, where media are concerned, is money.
Newspapers, television and publicity are relentlessly in search of
a larger audience.[6] The field of ratings research, which will determine the distribution of profits, is a controversial one; rivalry
between media has generated fanciful methods of evaluation. Yet,
despite instruments as sophisticated as the so-called 'people
meter' which should indicate who is in front of the television set
at any one time and even measures peoples' attention span, the
real people behind the statistics are in danger of being neglected.
Media are not interested in understanding what readers/viewers
feel, they merely need a 'thermometer' for measuring the foresee-
able benefits and share them. Theirs is an arithmetical logic which
has nothing to do with social practices experienced by concrete
agents. The illusion that public opinion might be easily fooled by
publicity or propaganda has been long abandoned. The most
refined techniques are uniquely used to decide between competitors and are not meant to provide social scientists with objective
data.[7] A humorist has said it is now proven beyond a doubt that
smoking is one of the leading causes of statistics. In other words,
it is because there is a sharp competition between them that the
tobacco industry finds it necessary to take a census of customers.
Let us take the statistics for what they are: a financial indicator,
a quantification of answers given to precise questions which are
not intended to reflect, in any way, audiences' feelings, interests
and preferences.

All such arguments about statistics do not imply that they

are negligible; on the contrary, they can help us detect hidden trends in the evolution of audiences and make us correct prejudiced opinions. There is, for instance, a feeling that radio listening is an increasingly declining habit particularly among the young. However, statistics suggest that, after a fairly rapid fall in the 1960s when people bought television sets, radio attendance grew slowly and has been surprisingly high since the beginning of the 1980s: listening and viewing coexist very easily at the end of the twentieth century. Is that enough, do statistics point out a 'fact'? Of course not, since the situation is much more complex. If we look at their schedules, we see that both radio and television tend to broadcast the same sort of programmes, namely rap and other kinds of pop music. Statistics signal a tendency. They cannot say more and they do not answer the final question: why? Is it that radio has been borrowing the hits of the small screen to pull an audience in? Is it, on the other hand, that television imitates radio to cut down on expenses? Or, alternatively, is the flow of pop so overwhelming that no section of the media is able to resist it? Statistics do not encompass that kind of query and we will not find a solution unless we look for systematic relationships among diverse aspects of viewers'/listeners' behaviour.

A final point which must not be forgotten is that percentages are weapons used in the competition for easier sales to advertisers. When cable television was launched in the United States, in 1970, its promoters were keen on convincing everybody that most households would be soon equipped; the start was very quick and the companies believed they could project the initial results into the future; they did not cheat on their potential customers but they organized their statistics so as to give the impression of a permanent, irresistible growth whereas a different presentation of the same elements would have anticipated a decrease in growth, which actually occurred after a decade. In that instance, as in many others, statistics were biased because they aimed to demonstrate something.[8]

What, then, is to be done with statistics and percentages? First of all, avoid what is patently obvious: we do not need a detailed statistical survey to guess that those Londoners who attend the Barbican or the National Theatre probably buy the *Independent* and listen to Radio 4 and it sounds a bit ridiculous to quote statistics to prove that the peak hours for television are from 8 p.m. to 10 p.m. or that elderly people spend more time in front of their television screen than do middle-aged people.

A second rule might be that we must adapt statistics to our aims. In many cases, a rough evaluation is sufficient; historians have proved that in around 1610, every week, some 20,000 Londoners went to the theatre in winter. A bit more? A bit less? It does not matter. The mere notion that about one out of ten inhabitants of the city was a theatre buff suffices to point out an important social trend. It is true that this is a remote period in history, but things are not very different nowadays; a rough estimate, superficial though it is, is often more telling than a detailed account. After fairly rapid growth in the years between the beginning and the middle of this century, cinema attendance grew more slowly or even stagnated in the 1950s. It has continued to decline until the present day. Is that not enough to make us evaluate the general trend of film production and consumption during the twentieth century?

It is true that more precise figures are sometimes useful but mostly for their critical value. Common sense suggests that television watching increased significantly during the Falkland Islands conflict or the Gulf War. To what extent? Since statistics are unable to distinguish between those who switched on their set and went to sleep and those who watched day and night, we do not need more than a rough evaluation which tells us, for instance, that, on the first two days of the Gulf War, television doubled its impact. As news services were entirely given over to the war, there were complaints. Assessments are worth noticing. BBC radio got 700 calls of protest against 100 calls of appreciation and there were about 2000 calls criticizing BBC television. The figures look small but very few other outbursts of dissatisfaction were ever so strongly manifested; we are not allowed to say that there was a 'serious' discontent but factual data signal a reaction (Against what? War itself? the broadcasting of war? A break in habits?) which should be analysed in the general context of the war. In such a case, statistics do not inform. They require the researcher to enlarge their enquiry.

Statistics aim at producing generalities, they determine a limited number of possible attitudes and classify a population according to these predetermined criteria. There is no objective fact in this field but there is an agreement between those who want to divide the market among themselves and accept the artificial verdict of statistics. When working for the media, statisticians have high standards of precision and low standards of fact because they are not seeking an audience beyond the media themselves. Statisticians tell stories even when they believe they do not tell them. They think that the crucial factor is measurement and they forget that they cannot separate their knowledge and the world because they are part of the world. Statistics are invaluable for they remind us that we belong to audiences: it is we who buy newspapers, read adverts, watch television. We tend to see 'the public' as an alien group of news consumers but, by stressing reactions different from or similar to ours, enquiries reinsert us amid the anonymous crowd without which there would only be individual, unrelated and erratic cases.

'We need to know more about our clientele'

There is something fascinating about statistics. They permit the drawing of graphics which seem to 'photograph' the public and to quantify its mood, tastes and habits at different times. Yet, if they are interested by the purely notional audiences that mathematicians construct for them, programme suppliers know very well that these statistics tell them little about the social identity of their customers. 'We need to know more about our clientele' has recurrently been presented by a good many media enterprises as their leading motto while, in fact, they do little to better comprehend it. Some media concentrate on a limited, easily identified public. There are magazines for hunters or anglers, there are local or thematic radio and television programmes aimed at specific audiences, but, even in this context, those in charge of 'visualizing' the public and conceptualizing its demands lack precise information. The history of the press, in past periods, is filled with evidence of repeated attempts made by journalists to get in touch with the readers; 'popular' newspapers, in the first half of the nineteenth century, addressed their clientele directly: 'You will recollect, my friends, we told you that .... And now, fellow countrymen, let us call your attention ...' When halfpenny papers blossomed at the end of the century, editors were keen on guessing what their readers wanted. Between the wars, Hilda Matheson, Head of Talks at the BBC, aimed at convincing her colleagues that 'the person sitting at the other end of the microphone expects the speaker to address him personally, simply, almost familiarly, as man to man'. These examples do not 'demonstrate' anything, they simply underline the banal truth that it is vital but extremely problematic for the media to take their audience into account.

At the time when Matheson was expressing her conviction with clumsy metaphors, philosophers, expanding on premises established by Max Weber, stressed the fact that any situation of communication is a social situation.[9] We shall come back later to the messages and their content. Let us consider, for the moment, that a message is a collection of signs whose purpose is to relate a group to another group or to parts of its environment. Understanding that a message is a message, not a chancy set of unrelated signals, is a complex operation which can be performed only when the addressees interpret the context from which the message has been generated. In an act of communication, the part of the listener is not passive. All messages are sent with gaps or approximations. It is up to the receivers to interpret the clues and to forge appropriate connections so that the part they play greatly transcends the mere effort of comprehension. To take a very simple example, anyone must possess a good level of understanding to spot a title while passing a stall or identify a theme while channel-hopping and then decide whether they will buy the paper or watch the programme.

Reception theories (which attempt to account for the way people listen to and understand programmes), have clarified issues that media mongers have long been exploring without acknowledging what they were doing. It is now wholly admitted, in editorial offices, that the purpose of newspapers, speeches or broadcast programmes is not simply to convey information or express opinions. Messages do not reproduce elements of the world, rather, they produce these elements and it is necessary, for readers or viewers to catch them, to be aware of the context in which they are developed; otherwise, people get only unrelated bits of reality which they soon forget. While reading or watching, users do not stop producing hypotheses which are tested in the text for confirmation or disconfirmation. As a process it provides for a gradual construction of meaning, which consents to interpret and include in a narrative syntax every motive or incident.

Cultural studies, influenced by deconstructionism, tends to stress the changes in the reception situation which characterize the end of the twentieth century. Readers/viewers, it is assumed, are all the more obliged to exercise their capacity of interpretation in that they are surrounded by more and more different messages. This is an interesting assumption for which there is no 'proof', for we cannot decide whether people, half a century or a century ago, were offered few messages. At the end of the last century, there were already a great many newspapers (in fact more titles than in the present day) and the streets were covered with posters An alternative hypothesis is that messages are all the more complex when they are less related to the addressees' immediate concerns. Such is the case with foreign information, with abstract problems like economy or with adverts. For example, an advert for a British bank showed four people, possibly the members of a family, playing golf indoors by trying to hit a lemon with an umbrella into cardboard rings on the carpet; the caption read: 'Indoor pastimes for people with a large mortgage and no special rate'. You have to ponder a bit to realize that there is no explicit connection between the text and the picture and you have to 'integrate' them before you come to the conclusion that this is an advert for a bank which offers low mortgage rates.

When they began, all media addressed a limited audience to which they diffused simple news. The early newspapers were often a single sheet aimed at a precise public and when the BBC began broadcasting there were nine separate stations which reached a local or regional population. The problems changed when audiences widened and when it became necessary to deal briefly with complicated issues instead of expanding on local problems. In addition, most media have long been depending heavily upon adverts which, quite often, are rather sophisticated and oblige the reader/viewer to make an effort in deciphering their message. Newspapers have received half of their revenue from advertising since the middle of the eighteenth century. The first Spanish daily, *Diario noticioso* (Informed Diary), launched in 1758, was divided into two halves – news and advertisements; in the same period a modest magazine, the *Salisbury Journal* printed some 1500 adverts every year. Broadcasting followed the same track. America's first radio station went on the air in 1920; two years later a Queens real estate company was the first to pay money for an announcement about an apartment block it was selling. In Europe, commercial radios such as Radio Luxembourg began to broadcast as soon as there were enough wireless sets. Sponsoring started on television about the time the medium was becoming a widely diffused means of information. Advertising and media have developed simultaneously, over a long period of time and they have influenced each other. The kind of participation that adverts require from audiences has affected the media.

It is therefore no wonder that editorial staff are sensitive to the capacity of their audience to transform the signals sent out by texts or programmes into messages. Yet, such a concern, whose increasing importance is perceptible in the curricula of communication or advertising schools, in the instructions given to journalists and broadcasters, in the yearly analysis of audiences, does not teach us very much about media consumers. To a large extent, the reader/response theory which we have just examined is mostly interesting for what it tells us about the worries or uncertainties of media producers; Hilda Matheson cared about her listeners, but she had few doubts about the fact that, if the messages were correctly composed they would be heard. Her optimistic vision has been dethroned by a critical construct which differentiates between possible ways of deciphering media messages but does not enlighten the actual practices and habits of audiences.

Is that to say that the media have no opportunity to know more about their clientele? Many regular readers/listeners personally address their favourite medium. In the eighteenth and nineteenth centuries it was not unusual to write to a magazine and give information or formulate criticism; in the 1930s, the BBC sometimes received two thousand letters a week and all television channels are regularly telephoned by faithful correspondents. These documents are often of paramount interest. They explain what people have chosen, how they have interpreted it, how they would have liked it to be handled, yet, little, if anything, is made from this input since a close study would require much time and effort, while an inquiry commissioned to a public relations office is quickly achieved and can be oriented according to the interests of its instigator. Here lies a wonderful source of information which has hardly been sampled[10] and is likely to modify our image of media audiences.

Sociologists must clearly distinguish between the specific aims of media which use statistics to prove that they reach huge audiences, and the requirements of social studies. Sociologists are sometimes obsessed with the idea that there is no 'science' without quantified and therefore comparable data. Statistics are sometimes useful but they reflect the concerns of those who have compiled them and when a query is slanted, the answer is necessarily biased. However vague it is, media have a notion of what their public consists of; it is important for us to know how they count their flocks and to what extent they see them as 'co-creators' of their programmes. But this refers to the media and their policy, not to their public.

THE USES OF MEDIA

What are media used for? A standard answer would be that they attempt at informing, entertaining and convincing. Do their consumers see them from the same angle? Many inquiries suggest that they do and they tend to characterize the media that they use according to the three above-mentioned criteria. But, if we check the questionnaires, we realize that, more or less implicitly, the media force these norms upon those who are interviewed; information, entertainment, influence all belong to the realm of effects. Is there no other procedure likely to reveal the functions of the media?

Sociologists know that interviewing those involved in a practice is not necessarily the best way of understanding what they actually do. However, enquiries about television viewing, without 'telling' one anything precise, provide thought-provoking insights into peoples' habits.[11] Many viewers when interviewed confess that they watch for several hours a day but usually at only a low level of involvement; they claim to view mainly for relaxation but stress the fact that they actively choose their programmes; they notice that new channels have flowered but signal no fundamental change in what or how they watch. Interestingly, they classify the programme types into categories similar to those which are used for print media but they conceive of television as something totally different which, despite the increasing number of channels, is less 'segmented' than the press. In short they conceive of television as 'theirs'. They realize how complex their relationship with the medium is but the questions which they have to answer do not offer them the tools or clues which would enable them to analyse their experience.

Beyond the market model

The trilogy of information/entertainment/influence is based upon the market model central to capitalist economy. It postulates, on the one hand, 'goods' such as news or pastimes and on the other, the customers who need or want them. The mass media are the channels through which these conveniences are provided to those who desire them. Marxists stress the ideological function of the media, a vast 'apparatus' in their vocabulary, which contribute to maintain consent; liberals emphasize the liberty of choice guaranteed by the variety of media and the harsh competition which opposes them, but all reason within the market paradigm. A significant aspect of these theories is that they treat the majority, if not the totality of the readers/viewers as a unique audience made up of generic, interchangeable users. The diversity of languages may limit the circulation of news but, generally, audiences are considered inside the political boundaries of the different states. They are, in practice, national audiences which national newspapers, national programmes and national networks try to reach.

The market model is not a newly contrived one. It can be traced far back in past centuries. In the first half of the nineteenth century, novelists began to use newspapers as a literary device, documenting thus the importance and various functions attributed to the press in modern societies. Edgar Allan Poe is especially revealing in this respect, he often introduced his own stories as texts written for a newspaper: 'In an article entitled "The Murders in the Rue Morgue", I endeavoured to depict some remarkable features...' (*The Mystery of Marie Rogêt*, 1842): daily newspapers are a major resource in Dupin's battle against the evil and he is keen on reading them very carefully: 'I procured, at the various newspaper offices, a copy of every newspaper in which, from first to last, had been published any decisive information in regard to this sad affair' (ibid.); it is thanks to his close scrutiny of rare magazines that the detective spots the killer orang-outang of the rue Morgue. Are we bound to take Poe's writings at face value? Are novelists especially in touch with their period? Can their stories serve as accurate indices of social movements? Poe spent his life seeking the chance to own a magazine and run it according to his own editorial preference. He raised the art of sensationalism to perfection and fooled a number of credulous readers with newspaper hoaxes, but his attempts to be involved with periodicals were successive failures and his literary descriptions of papers are totally fictitious. Even today, no newspaper would publish as precise and detailed an account of a murder as is the case in *The Murders in the Rue Morgue*. Expanding on the pattern delineated by Poe, films or novels stress important facts by interspersing their accounts with supposed articles or sensational front pages: 'The early editions of the evening papers had startled London with enormous headlines; *A message received from Mars*', Wells tells us in *The War of the Worlds* (1898). According to films or novels, people are intent on scrutinizing media, canvassing adverts from newspapers, begging for more and more information; it is a perfect illustration of the classical market theory, and the fact that it has pervaded literature or audiovisual productions shows how deeply rooted it is in the common vision of social intercourse.

The press or television are often spoken of as if there were a standardized press, or a unified television. The huge variety of newspapers, radio and, more and more, television networks is ignored. Local newspapers are perceived as by-products printed on old-fashioned machinery, filled with reports of courts, town councils, and jumble sales. Local radio is said to merely deliver news regarding the neighbourhood. We are concerned here neither with defending local media networks nor with deciding whether they provide more entertainment than on the national scale. These topics will be dealt with in the next chapters. However, what we must note is how difficult it is to combine the notion of a national audience with the impressive number and variety of provincial publications. With around 1800 titles, British local daily and weekly newspapers by far outnumber national publications.[12] I mention the press since it is often thought that the advent of radio and television has upset the market by developing the impact of advertising. In fact, long before the broadcasting era, many local newspapers already combined substantial circulation figures with high levels of advertising revenue. It is not because things have changed that conventional models, particularly the market model, have become inadequate. They have always been insufficient because they are partial and exclude vast areas of social relationships within which we find dynamics unaffected by the trade of news and entertainment.

The dominant model prevents us from fully observing what is happening because, due to its abstract logic, the point of view of the consumer is prejudiced and partially ignored. We had better give up starting from a theory and consider how people decide to adopt a medium, how they begin to make use of it and how they turn it into a routine.

Media and socialization

Two of the 'founder fathers' of German sociology, Ferdinand Tönnies and Georg Simmel were anxious to understand what characterized socialization. It has long been recognized that man is a social animal. This was even a basic assumption of western philosophy already clearly expressed by Aristotle which, however, does not explain how human beings socialize. We all belong to a family, from which we inherit our name and individuality and to a nation-state which defines us in terms of citizenship. Whilst acknowledging these basic characteristics, Simmel and Tönnies wanted to find out how, wittingly or unwittingly, people are much more than they are said to be, even when they fully accept pre-established categories. Passports, which document our filiation and nationality, overlook our identity. We have still other facets to our personalities, some of which last a lifetime, some of which are short-lived. The two German sociologists phrased their answers in seemingly different terms. Tönnies emphasized the importance of exchange relations, Simmel stressed the centrality of individuals. There was yet a common reference in their analysis. Simmel believed that there is a permanent conflict between individuals and society and that the former struggle to develop their potentialities against the rules that the latter imposes but he also believed that, if individuals want to be differentiated, they tend also to co-operate, the very fact of interaction being the beginning of society. As for Tönnies, he detected a society in any form of contractual exchange between men.

Starting from different premises, the two academics converged in stating that any relationship between people may initiate a sociation, provided these people share, while they act together, common concerns, customs, knowledge, pride or shame. Tönnies felt that the most obvious forms of human organization such as family or nation are not necessarily 'societies' for they are often suffered passively by their members; society, in his view, begins when the pre-established boundaries between individuals (clan, nation, etc.) become less significant, the neutralizing of differences and the development of voluntary exchange making people feel connected to each other while remaining independent. The interest of Tönnies' approach and what makes it invaluable for our study is that it finds elementary sorts of sociation in exchanges as simple as a conversation and considers antagonism, rivalry, hostility to be factors of cohesion as important as friendship or collaboration: any kind of relationship in which several people are implicated and which is oriented towards an aim contributes to creating society.[13]

The adoption and use of media are activities in which ephemeral sociations coalesce and disappear. This is something we do not estimate as its true value. As we are surrounded by media, we do not measure the part they play in our life. Let us leave our time and country to look at other locations and periods. Newspapers or audiovisual equipment are relatively cheap. Money is seldom an obstacle to our buying them. When they came onto the market, they were expensive, and, what was possibly more embarrassing, people could not see how they could integrate this new expense into their budget. A collective purchase was the best solution but it entailed real, assiduous collaboration. Many texts document the acquisition of a weekly newspaper by a group of people in the first half of the nineteenth century. Some historians calculate that, around 1830, there were some twenty readers for any copy of any radical paper, which implied a rather complicated organization, the readers being obliged either to gather in one person's home to read it or to circulate it. Today, the price of a radio or television set frequently exceeds the annual salary of an African worker; if, in countries like Nigeria or Ghana, the number of listeners is increasing considerably, it is because people unite to buy a receiver. Acquisition is merely the first step in a troublesome process, for the use of broadcasting equipment requires various forms of coactivity. Take this account of the way in which one British family tried to hear a primitive radio:

> My brother used to put the earphones in a basin and the sound was amplified by it. I can vividly remember the family crowding round and listening with their ears all close to this basin on the table. The sound must only have been very faint, but it meant that more than one person could listen at a time.[14]

Today, there are loudspeakers but there are other complications. Think of Africa: power does not reach large areas of this continent, batteries are necessary for radio or television sets and their management entails a degree of co-operation as difficult as the amplification of the old earphone. We do not need to go that far. When cable television started to operate in Europe, in the 1980s, people living in poor areas could not afford the connection to the transmitting station and they often joined forces to hire this connection.

Tönnies opened up urgent problems of socialization around the self, the other and their interaction. He very carefully distinguished between predetermined groups, families for instance, or neighbourhood groups, and conventional groups. The different examples mentioned above do not contradict but modulate his opinion. The case of the British household quoted above emphasizes the different parts played by the members of the family; short though it is, the testimony reveals an amalgam of competition and co-operation; the interplay between parents and children, sisters and brothers is momentarily modified while they are listening. The situation in many parts of the Third World is even more suggestive; in Black Africa, newspapers sell almost exclusively in urban areas; rural populations, whose relationships are largely based upon direct verbal communication, initiate a new kind of collaboration when they join forces to buy a television set.

The origin of socialization, in its various, changing forms, is, Tönnies explained, economy and particularly trade. Our last example supports his assumption that it is often the lack of money which leads people to combine their means. But money is not the decisive factor in our British family, or in other situations common in Africa. Think of cinema as it works in rural areas of Black Africa: there, the seats do not cost much because the premises are going to ruin and because the audience is only shown newsreels full of fat politicians or wealthy white ladies, and then lousy B movies. Still people gather in these places because it is the only possible joint entertainment for them, a way of getting out of the home and brightening up a dull life.

The power of symbols

The law of the market states that people co-operate because they lack money. In other words, consumption – a projected consumption – is the origin of their grouping. Is that all? If economy is involved in its formation, the group is also rooted in non-economic values: it is because they anticipate some advantage, however vague it is, that people unite to get a newspaper, or a receiver. While acknowledging his debt to the Germans, C. Wright Mills, the American sociologist, criticized them for underrating the importance of beliefs or conventions in the setting-up of short-lived groups and he emphasized the part played by symbols, notably by a language, in the interaction process which characterizes these communities. Buying a radical paper, in Britain, in the 1830s, was a political demonstration, the 'unstamped papers' (those which didn't pay tax and therefore weren't given an official stamp) were outlawed. Those who distributed them or even read them could be prosecuted. This historical allusion brings out a permanent function of media which, in critical situations, help people to clarify their position. Practices create new links by the manipulation of objects in shared situations.

Even in western, industrial societies, this role may be highly relevant. It has been shown that television played a crucial part in the Los Angeles riots of 1992; minority groups, living in isolation, began to have contacts, then to demonstrate in the streets, after they had realized, via the television, how badly treated they were by the local police: a series of news bulletins made them become aware of their humiliation. The symbolic function of the media is more obvious, if not necessarily more decisive, in dictatorships. Remember the part radio played in the evolution of Eastern Europe. It is not because of what was revealed, for those who tried to receive programmes broadcast from western Germany or America did not understand the words: they were rock fans. As the communist governments did not tolerate music which escaped classical dominant-tonic harmony, all those humming blues notes participated in articulating a general mood of dissent. The underground press also played its part in weakening the regime in the former Soviet Union and in the countries behind the Iron Curtain. *Samizdat* (an abbreviation for 'independent' or 'self-made publications') harshly criticized government, army and bureaucracy, but what they said was known to everybody. The decisive action was not to learn something from them but merely to have them. By getting a copy, any citizen signified their adhesion to the community of those who did not accept the state of things. Possession or diffusion of *Samizdat* reinforced a sense of shared identity of will and created a delineation between those who affirmed that the system could no longer work and those who preferred to ignore it. *Samizdat* illustrates the role of words in the formation of an audience. After the death of Stalin, terror was replaced in the former Soviet Union by the oppression of communist leaders, police and time-servers. The underground press attempted to find 'a proper word to name each thing'. It threw the ideological formulas out of its pages and contrived a new vocabulary. Its readers recognized each other, they affirmed that they partook in the same hostility to the rule-makers by avoiding the words 'brotherhood', 'unity', 'socialism', 'proletariat' and speaking of 'democracy', 'parliament', 'national will' and 'national sovereignty'. People did not use these words as passwords, as secret signs of recognition. They thought, they behaved differently because theirs was a new vocabulary. What existed between them, for a few years, was a community of thoughts and attitudes.

It is what Mills has in mind when he labels symbols the 'directing pivots' of social behaviour.[15] People who wear the same clothes, go to the same places and use the same words have something in common. They function as a precarious, moving community. Circumstances, in the former Soviet Union, were exceptional. It is clear that the underground press contributed potently to linking together disparate elements within a divided, demoralized country and was an important agent in the development of a radical opposition. What happens in less dramatic periods? A glance at post-communist Eastern Europe is revealing: in the void created by the fall of the old system, people were looking for an alternative culture; media, especially the radio, were crucial in diffusing ideas, slogans, formulas (call them what you will) that the younger generation, deprived of any political training, was able to catch and exploit. The rebuilding of a public ethos depended upon the formation of groups around symbols diffused by the media.

This is by no means a novelty. Dictators, in the first half of the twentieth century, believed that media would help them in making people debate and assimilate the lineaments of a national identity. Later, governments of third world countries thought that, in the same way, they would be able to break the isolation and indifference within which their fellow citizens were enclosed. Evaluating the impact of the media in the transformation of developing areas is almost impossible. It is no surprise that programmes on agricultural innovations broadcast in central Africa have no practical result since, for many reasons, the listeners cannot understand them, even if the vocabulary is simple. However, we are not interested in the content of these programmes, which we will return to later. We are only speaking of the aggregating effect of media: there is no doubt that radio and, to a lesser extent television, have always worked efficiently in giving rise to encounters between people who would otherwise have stayed apart.

The most visible communities are what we can call 'global communities' like nations, classes and tribes, which have a certain degree of permanence and stability and, very often, also have institutions. There is still a danger of overestimating the cohesion of these communities which are mostly frameworks in which other groups, sometimes institutionalized, more often fluid and ephemeral, come out, overlap and vanish. Society, as we understand it, according to Tönnies' assumption, is a permanent contact and interaction between unrelated groups which, nevertheless, influence each other since their members participate, simultaneously, in different aggregations. Life in communities, however spontaneous they are, relies on the possibility of communication about something to all participants. In all groups, be they totally transient, we find a collection of data, true or false, embellished or simplified, which enables the members to come together and strike up conversations, frequently purposeless ones, but always necessary, since they make up the soundtrack, the background fabric behind their collective actions. This cluster of facts, images and memories is partially forged by the associates and it comes, as well, from outside, especially from the media.[16] Instead of focusing on the influence media exert on individuals, we have questioned the relationship they create; co-operation, in this respect, is not a secondary aspect of the use of media. It becomes its most significant outcome. Sharing the same means of information, circulating them, discussing them creates an attachment to the group as a whole. In this respect, the content of media is important but less in itself than through the unifying effect it provokes.

Domination through media

Let us again visit the British family we left gathering around an earphone in a basin. We do not know how many of them were present, but we see that one of the brothers took the lead, devised a manageable technique and, probably, manipulated the set as long as there was no loudspeaker.

When speaking of the relationship between the media and power, we think first of state power, for even liberal governments are anxious to secure some control over the means of information. This is a key issue which will be discussed in Chapter 3. But power is not practised only by constitutional or economically dominant institutions. It is exercised any time a person is submitted to the authority of another person and accepts their subjugation because it is seen as legitimate or because there is no way of resisting it.

Our family introduces us to a first aspect of power – expertise. The brother, here, is only a bit more clever or quick than his family but mastery and cleverness are often closely linked. Weber was extremely sensitive to the influence, in industrialized societies, of specialists who receive 'a professional training which unavoidably increases in correspondence with the rational technology of modern life'.[17] Many facts exemplify Weber's opinion: early radio or television sets were fragile and complicated, only trained people could use them; when their quality improved, some listeners were still unable to deal with breakdowns and had to call technicians or get help from another person. Before that, in the past century, those who were involved in buying a paper were generally illiterate. They relied upon those who could read. The point, here, is not that equipment is too sophisticated – the popular papers were printed manually and, today, manufacturers tend to make their products simpler and simpler. The forms of authority developed by the media are complicated because they have both an economic and an educational aspect. In western countries, where families are overequipped, breakdowns do not matter but, in poor areas, appliances cannot be replaced, they have to be tinkered with as long as possible. Repairers thus gain an enormous influence. They are not real experts, only skilled people who take advantage of the poverty and ignorance of their neighbours. Their efficiency is not identified as power, but, because they are in a strategic position, they add to the stream of authority circulating in the society, and have an unwitting effect on the distribution of insidious control and creeping authority in the system.

How did the man who was entrusted with reading the paper to his comrades behave? How did he choose the texts he would emphasize? Did he comment on them? Documentation is poor in this field for workers had no time to note their impressions. On the other hand, we have plenty of information about the uses of radio. In Mediterranean countries, Italy, Spain and Portugal, where television came late, there were few sets during several decades and those who owned them dominated those who wanted to hear. Unlike workers' leaders, these men were rich and liked writing so we can study their strategy. Priests invited their followers. They made them listen to broadcast sermons. Landowners gathered together their labourers and families and relatives. They subjected them to 'good' speeches, 'good' music and, sometimes they made their servants dance. Other testimonies show that domestic or agricultural workers were often fascinated by that voice coming from nowhere. Radio, when it was cleverly manipulated, was an indirect means of domination. Listeners were not automatically impressed by what they heard. In the above mentioned situation of collective listening, which still exists in many parts of Asia and Africa, what is significant is not what is said but the fact that a man, because he owns a rare, intriguing device, can summon those who live around him and impose his will upon them. Economy is not involved in the process, labourers will not work harder because they have been gratified with a concert. It is a mere assertion of force based on apparent goodwill: 'you need entertainment but I know better than you what is suitable for you, you will hear what I want you to.'

Within a few years, after the middle of the century, transistors changed the situation and buying a radio set became the simplest thing possible, at least in western countries. Did domination vanish with the distribution of cheap equipment? We need only look back at the British situation, in the 1920s and 1930s, to guess that this was probably never the case; thousands of testimonies tell us that there was great competition for the control of the radio set. Take the complaint of a lady, interviewed many years after:

> Only one of us could listen in and that was my husband. The rest of us were sat like mummies . . . He always had these earphones on. He'd be saying, 'I've got another one', but of course we could never hear it – you could never get those earphones off his head.

More recent research has demonstrated that, in working-class families, the use of the remote-control is a prerogative of fathers who do not stop channel flicking across programmes while their wives would like to stop on one and watch it; if the father is not in, one of his sons, generally the eldest one, substitutes for him.[18]

Media reactivate pre-established divisions. Gender is clearly at stake when men confiscate the earphone or the remote-control. They make their supposed skill felt. They signal, indirectly, that the equipment has been bought with their money. It could be rightly argued that many people will modify this unbalanced relationship: affluent families provide each of their members with a television set, everybody selects what they want to watch. But many other problems arise where economic difficulties have been solved. Conflicts arise about the viewing time allocated to children, or the location of appliances, or the volume. The mechanisms that operate in this field go much beyond practical issues. They are ways of defining one's position in a community as well as being entertained or informed.

Social rites

One of the most challenging paradoxes of the media is that they convey the same news, the same serials and the same adverts to populations which live in totally opposite contexts. This oddity has often been stressed: how is it that distressed Nigerians and well-off Germans are gripped by the domestic quarrels of fanciful Texan families? If we focus on content, there is no precise answer. We are obliged to refer to entities as vague as the appeal of luxury or exoticism. The Marxist conception of media, described as tools used by the ruling class to maintain the relations of production and reinforce its domination, is far from negligible but it applies to the products themselves – newspapers, magazines, posters, radio and television programmes, not to the response of the public.

In different climates and locations, people read magazines, look at posters and watch television. The testimonies of Mediterranean experiences mentioned above show that audiences get quickly accustomed to listening or watching; after a few Sunday mornings spent in front of the church or in the courtyard of the mansion, country workers and domestics willingly assembled to hear the radio. That was in the first half of the century but we do not need to go that far back: today, in east and south Mediterranean countries, shops are equipped with a radio which plays constantly. Customers, friends and passers-by stop and comment on what they have heard. In other societies, patrons or casual visitors find papers in pubs. Throughout the world, people have become used to acquiring their news from media and finding enjoyment in them. The consumption of newspapers and television has developed to such an extent that it is now customary, among social scientists, to consider it a significant social ritual.[19]

Let us begin with a banal observation: a person, before getting on a train, buys a newspaper; she or he has a hasty look at it and leaves it behind when getting off. Routine. But 'routine', 'ritual' are vague words which cannot be used unless we clarify what they mean for us. In the situation we have imagined, the newspaper might be a symbol (I purchase this newspaper, not that one, I unfold it while I am out but I expect little from it) and, as such, it would help the buyer to organize daily practices. Ritual has mostly a religious or civic connotation, we see it flourishing amid assembled groups, involving most of their members and asserting their cohesion. Military parades are a good example. Initially, they meet some need; in periods of international tension, they serve to prove that 'we are ready' but, once they have been established, they tend to perpetuate. Spectators attend them since they expect that they will take place and armies perform them since they are expected to do it. The main purpose of parades, in peaceful times, is to continue what has been done previously for, if they ceased, there would be a vacuum in the succession of programmed events. Now, media have their share in creating and then maintaining rituals. They announce and amplify routinized events but, more importantly, they introduce these events to readers/listeners who cannot, or do not want to be present, they give them a national or even international audience. Later, when the urgent impetus behind the celebration has been exhausted, its recurrent commemoration, always mentioned in media, becomes part of the rites of a collectivity. Cabinet reshuffles were announced, in nineteenth-century newspapers, but nothing symbolized the moment in which a new government substituted for an older one; one day, a newspaper published a photograph of the cabinet, an instant was fixed, a ritual was instituted, every cabinet had to be photographed, magazines, newsreels, television were bound to disseminate these images despite the fact that they were tediously similar and not particularly telling.

Media are filled with data and messages. Let us forget for a moment, what they say. Let us consider magazines printed, and television programmes broadcast in a language we cannot interpret. Every newspaper or news bulletin has its standard size and is offered in a standardized manner; they give a series of data, ordered according to unspecified rules, a certain prominence. Even for us, who, supposedly, do not understand the words, an interaction between successive items or questions constitutes steps in the progress towards the end. For the native public, which reads or watches them day after day, these pages or programmes act as a form of ritual. What matters is not that 'something has happened' but that newspapers are in stalls when workers rush back home or that the *Nine O'clock News* starts at nine o'clock. Apart from the topics they choose, the media involve their audience in a kind of rite easily mastered thanks to pre-established features such as their size and length or the relationship between words and images. Circumstances are evoked but the elements making up the story are not essential in themselves, at least not for an absent-minded observer, for it is only the performance which has to be taken seriously.

Routines

Rituals have a social function which is efficiently supported by media but their impact is not limited to the public sphere. Freud paid great attention to the rites that people inflict on themselves. He labelled 'repetition-compulsion' an impulse to repeat the same gestures or recreate the same situations and he interpreted it as a form of resistance, an innate tendency to revert to earlier conditions. Routine is, to a large extent, a response to the challenges of life. It involves a defiance towards unobtainable goals and a preference for those suitable for existing means. While explaining how some individuals create rites as a defence against the pressure of their environment, this thesis, derived from Freud, is not fully satisfactory for people are not wholly free to organize their rituals. They have to accept orientations common to the society of which they are members; it would be inappropriate to speak of 'rules' for there is no constraint, but individuals comply with habits which often pre-exist them and suit them.

Suburban neighbourhood studies, which were flourishing in the 1950s, revealed an amazing uniformity in the arrangement of private space in working-class areas – the number of inhabitants, scarceness of room and the position of windows and doors could explain the location of furniture but why was the furniture absolutely identical? Why were small objects, appliances and even souvenirs alike? A comparison with other periods (testaments and inventories provide precise evidence from past centuries) and other areas detects the same monotony in any homogeneous group. It might be assumed, then, that the internal disposition of homes is dictated by different factors, namely social status, stage in the family circle and residential proximity, all factors which are closely correlated, for financial resources, family outings and lodging are interdependent variables.[20] Settlement types and incomes determine the size of house and the spatial arrangement of furniture, including, of course, audiovisual equipment.

Inside dwellings, receivers and even newspapers, are not mere

instruments of information. Their location in the house profoundly determines the way in which families perceive them. The
walk that has to be taken to switch them on or to watch them
introduces them in a certain context, their relationship with the
other objects in the room influences people's perception. Such
appliances are, at least partially, disassociated from their function
and settled, we might as well say 'socialized', in a world of
domestic articles united by the 'style' of the home. What people
know, what their friends say, unquestionably influences their conception of media but it is only within their surroundings that they
experience them.

Any handling of media is, in some respect, predetermined by
the context which is itself affected by the social condition of the
user. The place where a newspaper can be comfortably read,
the set-up of broadcasting facilities, depend on external factors
common to a whole group of people, and dictate the way in which
they are used. Routine, in this sense, is an unwitting adhesion to
a community which exists inasmuch as a sense of identity
develops between individuals; some of these may establish a network of interrelationships; they may also have few, if any, direct
contact, but they are, nevertheless, liable to a certain conformity.
This word is not used here in a perjorative sense; by adapting to
their surroundings, people settle limited but stable exchanges.
They are aware of the way the others behave as it is what they
themselves do. They know when they can pop in and, if the
television is on, they watch as they would have watched at home.

Communicating through the media

Most social exchanges simply aim at creating contact. Questions
are asked, answers are given, but no real information is being
sought. Redundancy or noises fill up letters, telephone calls,
encounters. Noises consist not only of discrepancies between the
speakers' understanding, it is also the interference of radio, or
television, which intrude into the conversation, are heard for a
short while and then are drowned out by a new dialogue. Media,
which participate in ritualizing the events, therefore play a part
in developing the rituals of communication. Together with family
or weather, they offer infinite resources for starting and prolong-
ing a chat. As a 'mode of action', conversation requires a substance which is easily found in serials, soaps or quizzes; speakers
do not need to describe their feelings. Facts and characters are

mere references which serve to establish a common sentiment. This is what explains the long-lasting popularity of series such as *The Archers* or *Coronation Street*: they are pure pretexts but they are also highly predictable; people do not even need to hear or watch them, it is enough to know they have been running for decades and that large audiences are fond of them. Watching *Coronation Street* is like looking through the window: at a given time the characters will be on the screen, at a given time your neighbours will pass by; you can miss the former or the latter, you are sure, anyway, that they have been there, on the screen or in the street. Talking with a friend about them is not a risky business.

The reception of the media, especially those that are broadcast, is akin to situations we experience daily, for instance at work, or when we are driving: moments of relaxation, of dispersed attention are interrupted by sudden tensions. Except when they read or watch very seriously, people are content to pick up a few segments from a continuous flow. But what has been absorbed, however partial it is, will be reused in other circumstances, in friendly conversations, at parties, in meetings at work and, likewise, the successive moments of the conversation with friends or colleagues will, alternatively, be exciting and cool. Information borrowed from the media and daily concerns will constantly overlap.

In the first section of this chapter, we have suggested that the data collected by the media to 'photograph' their public are not relevant for sociological research, not because they are wrong but because they are meant to answer commercial, not sociological queries. In this section, it was argued that audiences cannot be reached through statistics but are given only through their practice since they are formed, preserved and transformed in countless transactions. Being social practices, the various encounters of readers/listeners with the media are better described in terms of association, community, authority and habits, in short, everything which observes people's relations with others. This is not to say that the use of media is a realization of individual freedom. Consumption is, in fact, determined by the context in which it occurs. It cannot be understood if this context is not taken into account. Circumstances change, of course, as time goes by and that is the reason why we are bound to see how audiences form throughout history.

HOW AUDIENCES FORM

Audiences, as well as readers'/viewers' choices and inclinations are not intrinsic and directly legible. They are constructed as objects of studies by media companies or by social scientists and there is always a danger, in research dealing with 'the public' or 'the readers/viewers', of contriving a generalized, abstract person, or body which does not give more information than what is already included in the premises. This is the reason why so many students prefer analytical descriptions which show how different publics function at the same time, impelling researchers to compare various patterns of relations between users and media and making them evaluate media, not for the representations they create, but for the intensity of response they evoke among their consumers. Still, sociologists cannot indefinitely pile up case studies or try to articulate the countless types of short-lived groups engendered by the handling of media. They have to suppose that behind the multiplicity of processes and agencies that interfere in everyday life, there is a possible continuity. Comprehensive notions, which are artefacts, emerge because they answer practical needs for at least minimal order, so that, however spurious it is, the concept of audience is necessary. But how can we deal with it? Our vision is often constricted by the assumption that the dissemination of each aspect of the media, statistically measured, is basic to the definition of audiences. Yet, how shall we differentiate those who read newspapers from those who watch television for they are, to a large proportion, the same people. There is interference between the different, heterogeneous manipulation of media at a given time and also through the years. Presenting this changing, unstable combination by way of linear direction would be misleading. History, understood as evolution, would not elucidate what audiences are today. The apparent unity we try to establish is, in fact, sporadic in character and discontinuous from moment to moment. But glances at the past can help us to make comparisons. By selecting a series of relationships between media and users, each with its own characters and problems, we shall be able to master and apply the notion of 'the public'.

An historical approach

History is exploited in media research because it is an evolutionary science concerned with tracing the complex development of habits in time. It would be absurd to deny that advances in technology modify the conditions of production and enforce new inclinations among those who consume a good, whatever its nature is. There is no doubt that, since the end of the eighteenth century, larger and larger numbers of people, living in various lands have been enabled to communicate with, and to be aware of distant countries which, previously, most of them would have ignored.

Radio is a good example of the accuracy of an historical explanation. Other examples might also be cited but radio, which became popular in a short period of time, provides us with a life-size experiment. At the end of the First World War there was, on the one hand, a great demand for entertainment and information. New exciting songs and dances from America were in popular demand. People were also longing for peace but the period was uncertain, confused and all newspaper readers during the war demanded more news, more quickly. On the other hand, companies, such as the Western Electric Company in Birmingham, General Electric and ATT in the US, Telefunken in Germany, which had made money by exploiting electricity or telephone services, were ready to invest in a similar service. The possibility of transmitting radio waves through space without wires had long been in existence, but the radio was considered to be an instrument of private communication, a sort of perfected telephone. No-one had envisaged that there could be a single centralized, anonymous transmitter and an enormous number of receivers. The propagation of radio was prodigiously rapid. In Britain alone, according to the available (and unreliable) figures, there were 600,000 licences in 1923 and more than two million four years later. Three factors were converging at the beginning of the 1920s: (1) technical devices, tested for two decades were completed during the war; (2) a vast amount of money was available and manufacturers were ready to risk it; (3) there was a potential audience. Radio, it seems, offers a 'model' which might be applied to other media.

The growth of the press, in the second half of the nineteenth century, was also influenced by the three decisive factors we have just delineated. Technical improvements multiplied, from the rotary press, which printed thousands of sheets per hour, to the Linotype on which pages were composed on a keyboard, instead of being assembled manually. Meanwhile, the telegraph and telephone speeded up the dissemination of news and modified the conception of information by concentrating on facts rather than opinion. With the introduction of new machinery, the costs of newspaper enterprises grew tremendously but a few entrepreneurs realized that newspapers filled mostly with succinct new systems and sold at a low price would gain a large readership and, consequently, a wide range of advertisements. Considerable investments resulted in huge profits, often reinvested in the development of popular Sunday magazines. In industrial countries, education was then progressing, compulsory school attendance enabled an increasing part of the population to, at least, read short, unsophisticated news, a growing demand made the circulation levels soar and the large majority of adults became used to buying daily newspapers.

Another crucial innovation was the inclusion of illustrations. Engravings were introduced in newspapers after 1880, photographs in 1910. Meanwhile, in 1896, cinema was invented. Over many years, scientists had been researching picture animation; once the problem had been resolved, moving pictures were immediately exploited. The inventors who lacked money and confidence were soon taken over by capitalist companies and film production was industrialized. Fifteen years after the first film, millions of people were flocking to the cinema.

The historical approach is interesting inasmuch as it pays particular attention to the stages of technological growth and to the unhesitating, swift reaction of capitalists who adapted easily to the circumstances. It also allows us to take into account other factors which were less conclusive but precipitated a generalized consumption of media. Speed was, for instance, a leading preoccupation during the second half of the nineteenth century, not only from a realistic point of view (time is money) but also from the perspective of imagination, speed being often associated with progress, discovery, expansion and liberty. With the new media, information arrived more quickly, people's horizons were widened considerably, those who did not travel were, indirectly, associated with the conquest of space. They read in their newspapers accounts of various explorations, they saw, on the cinema screen, aircraft which they themselves would never travel on. In this respect and in many others, media introduced isolated individuals to a symbolic space distinct from their ordinary world, creating thus an artificial whole, the media audiences.

A long-term evolution

I have stressed the historical approach for, even today, it is often
accepted uncritically. It is a simple approach and seems to tie in
with all available evidence and it provides an account of social
change over a long period. However, it is difficult to accept it at
face value.

To begin with, there are many inconsistencies in the application of such a model, and too many data which do not fit. The
most obvious concerns television. Whereas the other media were
adopted almost immediately after they were available to the
general public, some sort of reluctancy or hesitation can be
detected where television is concerned: it took five years of broadcasting for the number of television licences to reach one million
in Britain. Exceptions do not prove a rule – they oblige one to
revise it. Broadly speaking, it is true that capital investment
played an important role in the launching of new media, but a
closer inspection shows that, in many cases, entrepreneurs began
with no money and that some of them amassed a fortune out of
nothing. It is true that, in the United States, in Britain and in
other countries, powerful companies manufactured cheap radio
equipment, thus permitting workers to buy them. But in Italy,
where electrical industries were modern and rich, manufacturers
maintained high prices (in 1930 a radio receiver cost one-third of
the price of a small car) because they made more money with
expensive, hardwearing articles than with economically priced
fragile ones: the pure logic of profit led to opposite solutions in
different contexts. Despite what is usually called their 'industrialization', the media themselves are not industrialized goods; they
are products of large consumption made possible thanks to instruments manufactured by industry, which is rather different.

The historical approach suggests many connections by focusing on simultaneity but it is at risk of forgetting the importance
of change. Let us start with a simple case of misleading synchron-
ism. There was for instance a close relationship between the
growth of popular science fiction and the rapid growth of cinema.
Méliès would not have been so successful without the impact of
contemporary writers such as H. G. Wells, or other visionaries
who propagated the dream of galactic conquest on the later
generations of the nineteenth century. If futurist films and novels
reinforced each other for about a decade, after 1910 Méliès had
no successor and his genre disappeared, while written science

fiction prospered. The encounter was short-lived, it deserves a mention but the separation is also worth noting as it prevents us from drawing hasty conclusions. In the same way, all we can say about speed or about large horizons is purely speculative, statements of this kind being constructs which attempt to devise a simple, rational scheme out of a multiplicity of data. They are thought-provoking but do not prove anything.

The trouble with the evolutionary model is that it combines easily checked details (the beginning of broadcasting, various improvements in reception) and assumptions. One of the pillars of the theory is that there was a potential audience; in other words, since audiences grew very fast, as has been noted, it is supposed that people were ready to constitute a 'public': a circular argument of that sort does not tell us very much. When we look closer at the 'demonstration', we find that it borrows most of its argumentation from the mass-society conceptualization which we have already discussed at the outset. According to that idea, industrialization and the market economy have destroyed the dense network of personal relationships which existed previously; people have become equal, anonymous entities, governed more by impulse than conviction, whose rudimentary education will reduce culture to a lowest common denominator. We do not need to 'discuss' mass-society conceptions here; the only point we must emphasize is that they mix up number and mediocrity: if there are many readers/viewers, what they consume is necessarily bad; conversely, high circulation of newspapers and continuous broadcasting are disastrous because they reach large audiences. Different though they are, those who have developed, or are still developing this train of thought share a deeply rooted dislike of urban life and industrialized production. For them it is quantity which is synonymous with homogenization and impoverishment of culture.

Now, how do we know that readership was limited when newspapers were few and small? Around 1840 the circulation of stamped newspapers was about 10,000; at the end of the century, dailies sold millions of copies: the tremendous gap between these statistics seems to point to a revolution. But what about the unstamped newspapers and their circulation? By 1840 the sharing of newspapers was a common practice which multiplied the quantity of users. Exact statistics are lacking but, as has already been said, the number of readers or listeners, again in the 1830s, was around twenty for every copy. Some newspapers could reach

circulation figures of 50,000 and as there were many such newspapers, it has been conjectured that a total of four million readers/
listeners is not an unreasonable guess.[21] This supposition may be
excessive, but it still remains that many people were used to
getting something, either information, or entertainment, or
opinions, from the press. No spectacular change occurred when
the rotary press was invented. A pre-existing readership, which
had slowly expanded since the late eighteenth century, was the
matrix in which a new, enlarged readership expanded after 1840.
This is not to say that there was no change. We cannot help
observing a noticeable contrast between the newspapers stamped
on a cheap iron-frame press, which stressed deprivation, struggle
and violence and the manufactured ones which dealt with more
general, less controversial topics, but the fact that the style of
newspapers evolved over a half-century does not imply that the
press renewed its readership. There was, rather, a slow transformation. Various groups of readers, who were used to reading
different magazines, dissolved imperceptibly into each other,
establishing thus another relationship, more distant, less personal,
between the media and their public.

What happened in the middle of the nineteenth century was
not the birth of an audience; it was more an alteration of the
social norms which oriented the press and its clients. Before this,
the users of the stamped or popular press found their needs
expressed and sometimes answered in their newspapers; they read
about their own lives in them. On the other hand, the buyers of
industrially manufactured newspapers were introduced to other
worlds and concerns; they began to read for the pleasure of
reading, not to read about their own lives. This was an aspect
of what Weber called the disenchantment, or demagification, provoked by the dissolution of traditional, closely united communities. Oddly enough, little research has been carried out on the
progressive estrangement of readers from their papers.

A social mode

Theories which link the 'birth' of the modern press readership
with technological changes and urbanization are much too simple.
Innovation triumphed in this field because a pre-existing public
was already used to consuming newspapers. Is it possible to
extend to other media what has just been said? There is little
doubt that they all attracted audiences which had already

gathered for other purposes. Films were initially shown in cir-
cuses, wax museums, 'wonders of science' exhibits or playhouses,
interspersed with songs and dances, to working-class customers
who had little time off and were used to attending short, easily
understandable shows. In the 1910s, the nickelodeons, with their
brightly lit lobbies, their bands and the brief comic or dramatic
sketches that they offered were still akin to the music hall; in
other words, spectators discovered the cinema in a familiar context; cinema films were already fifteen years old, and audiences
had got accustomed to them when the first picture houses were
opened. Before the beginning of radio broadcasting, music was
performed in various societies or local bands and the gramophone
was much in vogue. Meanwhile, thanks to the rapid spread of the
telephone, which had been operational since the 1880s in Britain,
the United States and most industrial countries, people had
become used to listening to far away voices;[22] wireless audiences
grew rapidly in areas where the telephone was already currently
employed while in Italy, for instance, both telephone and radio
were adopted much later. As for television, whose audience
increased slowly during the initial period, it must be remembered
that, in the late 1940s, prices were high, wages low and that those
who had been obsessed with their radio during the war did not
want to give it up; after a few years, the number of licences
boomed. Contrary to what one might guess, those who bought a
set continued to listen to their radio and to go to the cinema,
which seems to indicate that consumption begets consumption.
In the 1980s, cable television surpassed the three national networks in the United States and it should be noted that it
developed chiefly where local radio stations were already
operating.

Admittedly, this is too cursory a comparison which presup-
poses a social homogeneity among users that has never existed;
workers went to the cinema at the beginning of the century
because it did not cost much, whereas only affluent people could
buy a television set in 1950. But what I would like to emphasize
is not the structure of audiences, it is the fact that no public is
created out of nothing. Our understanding of large-scale phenomena is often biased because nobody thought to observe them
before they became conspicuous so that the first data were collected once the process had been under way for some time; many
clues indicate that radio-listening was widespread at the end of
the First World War but no assessment was made before 1923; the

statistics for that year point out a burst of enthusiasm, which is illusory.

Instead of being strongly influenced, and even altered, by fashion or technical contrivances, media consumption is a form of culturally determined behaviour in which individuals settle a customary relationship with some means of information. The way people use the media varies enormously; although supply has been increasing throughout the past two centuries, there are still casual users on the one hand, and media addicts on the other. Quantity is not crucial, what counts is the competence possessed by all those who have introduced the media into their lives. Getting information or entertainment not from the neighbourhood but from far-away sources is a social habit which, after some time, becomes as much a characteristic of a given group as using public transport or living in multi-storey buildings. Media evolve and their clients consume them diversely, according to their appearance, cost and content, but the very usage of media has become a distinctive feature of modern societies.

A two-step process

Is it possible to be more specific about the emergence and progression of new, or much wider audiences when media diversify? The traditional idea, which stresses technical innovation and investment is so well accepted that little has been done to investigate further and see how people get acquainted to new means of information. The scarcity of preliminary research allows us to make only a few assumptions.

In the first volume of his *History of Broadcasting in the United Kingdom*,[23] Asa Briggs has collected all available information on the creation of the 'great audience' of radio. Those who bought radio sets, from 1923 onwards, were well-off people but we have noted that, in the six previous years, there had been many listeners who came from all sections of the population. Around 1920, there were no programmes; messages were broadcast partly by institutions such as the Navy but mostly by amateurs who tried to communicate among themselves. Radio technology had developed during the war and, in 1918, had become a fully integrated system of communication which turned out to be useless after the armistice. The large electricity corporations, which had manufactured radio equipment, and wanted to get rid of their stocks, sold them at bargain prices. Enthusiasts acquired the components and assembled them as well as they could; the receiver was not the domestic implement that it would later become, it was an instrument which served to speak and listen. These enthusiasts formed their own audience. They became a cohesive group cemented by a common passion, an empirical but effective mastery of radio waves, and a strong will to improve their skill. Even from an institutional point of view they were a social force; when the American government attempted to pass a bill securing the control of radio to the Navy, the Radio Relay League, an organization of radio amateurs, succeeded in opposing it. The pioneer age was closed by a joint effort from governments and electricity companies which imposed a public or private monopoly everywhere and began to prosecute licence dodgers. If the monopoly was enforced for economic and political reasons, it was also defended for functional motives: the waveband is narrow; long-distance reception is almost impossible unless signals are broadcast on a precise, constant wavelength. Monopoly thus meant the end of conversations between radio amateurs and the beginning of regular programmes. Listeners were no longer a group of enthusiasts, they were consumers.

This would not be an interesting case if it were exceptional. However, if we take it as a reference, we can observe the same two-step process in other fields. The 'pauper press' developed, in the first half of the nineteenth century, thanks to the joint efforts of amateurs who collected news reports, sometimes wrote articles, printed the copies on a hand-press and sold them; the readers participated in the making of the newspapers and set up an autonomous distribution system based on the enthusiasm of the producers/readers. Co-operation, which was a powerful integrating force for the workers, also contributed to encouraging reading practices among the poorest people. In the second half of the century, the industrialization of the press overpowered the hand-made newspapers so that people, instead of making their papers, were content to buy them.

Early cinematic equipment was rudimentary, it consisted of a wooden box, a lens, and a crank and was used first to shoot, then to project the film once it had been developed; skilful photographers were able to construct a camera, churn out short films and show them in fairs. It took almost a decade for spectators to be tired of the pure magic of moving images and ask for more sophisticated stories. Even so, many of those who attended picture houses kept on buying spares, assembling their own film cameras and making domestic films; video had widely extended the practice of private film-making but nobody would try to construct a video camera while, when cinema was young, amateurs were keen on creating their own material.

The high price of cathode-ray tubes should have prevented amateurs from building television receivers, but the impact of radio had been so strong that, in the second half of the 1920s, hobbyists attempted to make and operate their own transmitting devices. The problems involved in the production of stable images turned out to be too complex for individuals, however skilled they were, and most amateurs gave up before the Second World War, but the first decade of industrial research on television was marked by a close collaboration between fans and engineers.

In the above-mentioned cases, the period of enthusiasm was short-lived: what does it matter if people initially produced their newspapers, or films, or receivers if, in the end, they became mere consumers? It matters because, in each of these examples, fans started a trend. Statistically, the stamped press was of little importance compared to the unstamped one; it would have progressed at any rate in the second half of the century but it would never have given rise to mass consumption which was created by the fans of the unstamped press. Spain provides us with an impressive counter-example. In Spain, hand-made newspapers never prospered and even today, despite the democratization of Spanish political life, the circulation of daily newspapers is extremely limited and does not stand comparison with distribution in other European areas.

The 'amateur phase' establishes a substructure and creates an interest. It is a time when small journals flourish. In 1910, for instance, more than three hundred cinema magazines, mostly composed by amateurs, were issued throughout Europe. They aroused curiosity, and contributed to the definition of a specific vocabulary; at the same time, they were noticed by older publications which brought them to their readers' attention. Cinema, radio and television were commented upon before they were widely available because a few active, passionate people were paying a great deal of attention to them and were using them with excitement. As early as 1929, a Television Association was founded in Germany with the joint participation of hobbyists, technicians and journalists so that the latter, coming in contact with experts, became keen on informing their readers. It is surprising but significant to notice that there were numerous news-papers about television in the Berliner press around 1930.

Fans also played a decisive part in the propagation of new media inasmuch as they tested the equipment and contributed to its improvement. It was for these people that retailers of electrical goods started to stock receiver kits and, little by little, came to sell industrially manufactured sets. Amateurs participated mili-tantly in legitimating inventions or technical improvements at a time when they could not yet operate effectively. Traditional theories, which emphasize innovation and the role of businessmen able to detect a potential audience, account neither for the origins of this latent public, nor for the motives of its adopting new equipment. Assumptions about the two-step process are likely to bridge this gap; according to this hypothesis, technical or scientific novelties, which had not reached their full development, were simultaneously experimented with and sanctioned by the enthusi-asm of a minority; it is thanks to this minority that manufacturers were lead to jump from experimentation to wholesale production.

What has been said about television stresses the complexity of the process: a television-to-be benefited from the success of the radio and, simultaneously, contributed to reinforcing this success; listeners hoped they would soon be offered a 'videoscopy-set' and film buffs who could not yet get a domestic cinema bought what was closer to it, a radio set. The various media, which are competing against one another, are not exclusively rivals, they overlap. It is their differences and their similarities which encour-age people to compare their performances. The curiosity aroused by a single medium begets interest in other media.

The constitution of media audiences, such as those we can observe in our time, has been a long-lasting process. Historical inquiry can help to define who were readers of the first news-papers. But these people belonged to other, previously existing audiences, they did not come from nowhere. A new medium does not 'produce' its public, it attracts some sectors of an existing public and contributes to enlarging it by luring individuals who formerly had no interest in the field. Three centuries of growing practice have created a familiarity with the written or spoken means of information which we have incorporated into our daily lives as much as we have integrated the means of transport. Researchers can explore a particular audience, at a given time; however, from a sociological point of view, these publics are simply limited sectors of something which is not a countable entity ('the public') but an unstable, fluctuating set of people.

Observing audiences

Weber postulates that every aspect of human activity which involves choices can be illuminated by assuming that people behave rationally. Rationality is understood, here, in a special way: a decision counts as being rational if it is in fact well adapted to fulfilling a given end, even if the end itself seems irrational or if the agent is not aware of his/her aim. From this point of view, the first task of the sociologist is to understand the factors which motivate an action.

We began this chapter by looking at the statistics collected by the media producers. Precise and accurate though they are, these statistics cannot help us very much; those who pay for them care more for global data than for social analysis; they consider that numbers can describe 'their' public and that measurement is the most important variable in the definition of their policy. Given their aim, which is the expansion of profit, evaluated in sales, theirs is a rational calculation.

The trouble is that the rationality of media consumers cannot be brought into relation with the very simple standards of money; statistics miss the gradual nature and localized impact of social practices. Even as simple an experience as the daily use of a television set is, to a large extent, a fragmentary, fluid occupation. Many social determinants and particular situations induce a wide range of contrasting attitudes towards the media. Hence, the necessity of a micro-perspective which tests the choices of individuals or small groups, in a particular place and time, with regard to specific issues such as the scarcity or abundance of information, the relations of power, the pre-existing stock of knowledge. Starting from theoretical premises proposed by Tönnies, we have seen that media often turn out to be factors of social cohesion, accelerators of social life. Rationality, in this respect, consists of using media as signs, or symbols, and in creating a group identity around a medium. By maintaining a possibility for immediate interaction, the newspapers or broadcasting sets participate in creating a symbolic proximity.

However, we may be conceding that the subjective experience of using a given medium is something we cannot easily describe. While trying to go further, we must bear in mind the personal participation which is at the centre of the consumption of media and we must admit that exploring this participation is an unsolved problem for sociology. There is still another danger which is to discard any notion of larger units, such as, for instance, 'radio audiences between the wars' or 'television audiences today'. Contrasting with the micro-approach, we have therefore attempted to delineate a macro-perspective which maps different 'layers', or generations of media consumers, in connection with the advance of new media, in order to assess the relative idiosyncracy of each and see how all these groups, while being different, interfere with one another. We have stressed a long-lasting tendency, developed over three centuries, towards a widening of media audiences. We have also noted that, when they appeared, the new media were adopted and promoted by a limited group of enthusiasts who were more interested in technical performance than in the spread of information; this initial step, motivated by curiosity and hobbyism, was crucial for the introduction of media onto the market. It provided the impetus which convinced other customers to join and enlarge an already existing public.

Different logics have always interfered in the field of media use. They can be referred, respectively, to a desire for higher profits, an inclination towards collective activities and an interest in innovation. However different they are, these rationalities converge at one point which is the dissemination of information: media are made to tell something. But, before studying the contents of media, it is necessary to show that the readers/viewers are not mere consumers of news or entertainment. While coming together to read a newspaper or listen to a broadcast programme, audiences have a partially independent life which finds its pretext, not its cause, in the media.

NOTES

1 E. Durkheim, *The Division of Labour in Society* (1984, London, Macmillan), pp. 47–50.
2 M. Weber, *Economy and Society* (1978, Berkeley, Los Angeles and London, University of California Press), Chapter 2, paragraphs 9 to 12, esp. p. 26 ff.
3 Max Weber was, of course, well aware of the importance of the written press in a liberal economy; at the first conference of German sociologists, in 1910, he advocated a methodological study of periodicals and mentioned the importance of an

analysis of content up to its quantifying aspects but, for him, if the newspapers were a valuable source of evidence, they were not 'media'. Weber grappled again with the newspapers in *Politics as a Vocation* (1919) but, in this book, he was mostly interested in the ethics of journalism and the press did not command the position which most scientists today believe essential to social studies. This is a good example of the difference between the importance attributed to means of information such as documents and the significance given to the media by the scientific community. Marx used to say that societies do not raise questions that they cannot solve; conversely, when an answer cannot be put into words, neither can the question be put into words.

4 Good introductions to the research carried out to investigate the effectiveness of audience reaction measures in J. Lewis, *The Ideological Octopus: an Exploration of Television and its Audience* (1991, London, Routledge) and B. Gunter and M. Wober, *The Reactive Viewer: a Review on Research on Audience Reaction Measurement* (1992, London, John Libbey).

5 D. Chaney, *Fictions and Ceremonies* (1979, London, Arnold).

6 See I. Ang, *Desperately Seeking the Audience* (1991, London, Routledge).

7 The theory of sampling was defined by the Norwegian Kiaer in 1903. Archibald M. Crossley offered to apply it to test radio audiences in 1929; he founded the *Cooperative Analysis of Broadcasting*, with the participation of firms such as Procter & Gamble or Young & Rubicam and began his ratings in February 1930. The methods have become more and more sophisticated throughout the years but their bases are still those defined by Kiaer. For a history of ratings see J. Beville and H. Malcolm, *Audiences Ratings: Radio, Television and Cable* (1985, New Jersey, Lawrence Erlbaum Assoc.).

8 S. Tyler Eastman, S. W. Head and L. Klein, *Broadcast/Cable Programming Strategies and Practices* (1985, Belmont, California, Wadsworth Publishing Company).

9 A pioneer research in this field was A. Gardiner's *The Theory of Speech and Language* (1932, Oxford, Clarendon Press) a readable work which develops more along a sociological than a linguistic line. It has been revised and completed by J. L. Austin, *How To Do Things With Words* (1962, Cambridge Massachusetts, Harvard University Press) and J. R. Searle,

Speech Acts: An Essay in the Philosophy of Language (1969, Cambridge University Press).

10 A first attempt has been made by M. Pegg, *Broadcasting and Society, 1918–1939* (1983, London, Croom Helm).

11 P. Drummond and R. Paterson (eds) *Television in Transition* (1985, London, BFI); J. Fiske, *Television Culture* (1987, London, Methuen); K. Jensen, *Making Sense of the News: Towards a Theory and an Empirical Model of Reception for the Study of Mass Communication* (1986, Aahrus, Denmark, Aahrus University Press); K. Richardson and J. Corner, 'Reading reception: mediation and transparency in viewers' account of a TV programme' (*Media, Culture and Society*, 1986, vol. 8, no. 4, pp. 485–508).

12 C. Seymour-Ur, *The British Press and Broadcasting since 1945* (1991, Oxford, Blackwell).

13 F. Tönnies, *Community and Association* (1955, London, Routledge).

14 Quoted in P. Scannel and D. Cardiff, *A Social History of British Broadcasting, v.2, Serving the Nation* (1991, Oxford, Blackwell), p. 357.

15 C. W. Mills, *Power, Politics and People* (1963, Oxford University Press), p. 454.

16 P. Connerton, *How Societies Remember* (1989, London, Cambridge University Press).

17 M. Weber, *Economy and Society*, ibid. p. 366.

18 For radio, see Scannell and Cardiff, ibid., p. 357ff.; for television, see T. Bennett (ed.) *Popular Fiction: Technology, Ideology, Production, Reading* (1990, London, Routledge).

19 'Ritual Tasks', conclusion of *More Bad News* by the Glasgow Media Group (1980, London, Routledge & Kegan Paul); 'A symbolic mirror of ourselves: civic ritual and society' by D. Chaney in R. Collins (ed.) *Media, Culture and Society*, (1986, London, Sage, pp. 119–135).

20 See especially M. Young and P. Willmott, *Family and Kinship in East London* (1957, London, Routledge & Kegan Paul).

21 P. Holl, *The Pauper Press* (1970, London, New York, Oxford University Press), p. 124 ff.

22 I. De Sola Pool (ed.) *The Social Impact of Telephone* (1977, Cambridge Massachusetts, Cambridge University Press), p. 305 ff.

23 (1961, London, Oxford University Press), p. 18 ff.

2
Contents

In the previous pages we have often mentioned those thinkers who were afflicted, from the start, with a nostalgia for past culture which resulted in their measuring contemporary production, especially 'mass' production, by comparison with those of the past, and denouncing their total absence of meaning. For these people, who have been rightly called 'the lamenters',[1] the content of the media was intrinsically bad, it was only destined to lure the readers/viewers and make them accept the ideas of the ruling class. There is little doubt that mass media and propaganda are closely linked. However, is it enough to say that what can be found in the media is merely ideology or that the mass media are encouraging the demolition of culture? The critical vision is basically pessimistic. Sociology must not be either optimistic or pessimistic; its aim is simply to evaluate social relationships. We have seen that many social exchanges develop from a collective use of media. But these media are not only objects which can circulate. They have also a content and tell us something. We must now try to understand how people make sense of what they read in their newspapers, or see on television.

Any message goes from an emitter to a receiver and it is

tempting to follow the different stages in the process: someone (who?) makes something (what?) which influences (how) another person. Postmodernism, in its attempt to go beyond this simple, univocal transaction has coined a metaphor: it defines culture, and any aspect of culture (from cooking to kinship systems), as texts to be interpreted. Etymologically, the word 'text' is related to textile. A text, like a textile, is a combination of elements put together in such a way as to constitute an autonomous product. Using this very broad definition, neither the origin of the texts nor the nature of the elements are of paramount importance. The thing that counts most is that any text, although being a compilation of different elements, has its own identity. A book, a newspaper, a print (but also a household object or a film) are texts that their user deciphers and what we have to do is to determine *how* she or he does it.

As has already been said, the world of the mass media is a kind of intermediate sector between the concrete area where people act daily and the problems, or concerns, or worries which are present, important to them although they can only reach them obliquely; the media represent the transition from one sphere to the other; they provide a real experience, the experience of viewing or reading, which is also of an indirect, imaginary nature. There is something paradoxical in the work of the media; they add to the world in which we live a supplement which is both within and above it. In itself our world is already a whole, an omnipresent plenitude. And yet the media attempt at replacing it. Not only do they reduplicate it but, in many respects, they substitute it: a good many people watch television to see what they could witness in the street.

INFORMATION

In the jargon of cinema studios, an image is called 'a take'. It is something that has been taken, or cut out of the universe to be printed on a film. An Argentinian novelist, Bioy Casares has written a story, *Morel's Invention*, which is a metaphor of all the media. An unidentified runaway lands on an island where he feels obliged to go unnoticed; he observes the inhabitants and remarks that, week after week, they perform the same gestures; after a while, he realizes that they have been 'swallowed' by a film camera, which has 'sucked' their blood and flesh and now projects their image; they look like human beings, but they are

mere effigies which will endlessly repeat what they did the previous week. This sounds a bit odd but think how our image can
be captured on film for posterity.

Mass media and everyday life

Different though they are, all the mass media capture and reveal
aspects of the world as it exists before the eyes of the journalists
or cameramen. It is clear that, in the main, the newspapers are
filled with information about current affairs and that posters
present us with objects we could buy. The prodigious impact
that films won almost immediately would not have been possible
without the widespread idea that they were able to catch and
preserve the reality. Initially, the movie camera was conceived as
a clever device contrived to observe the successive stages of
locomotion and it was popular demand that transformed it into
a witness of the universe. The first films were films of real events
and, around 1905, outnumbered fictional ones; later, feature films
flourished for commercial reasons that we shall analyse later.
Today, radio or television programmes are mostly made of news,
reports, documentaries or talks and debates about what is happening at present. It seems that audiences, when they can make
their selection, choose information rather than fiction. With 'pay
per view', people who have access to the cable television decide
what they want to see instead of accepting what they are offered
by a network; their preference for news is so obvious that 'pay
per view' has been renamed 'pay for event'; some noisy competitions have been watched by twelve million spectators whereas
fictional hits do not even reach one-fifth of that figure.

The media are often defined by the fact that they provide
'information' but, then, this term is used in a specific, partially
misleading way. In fact, when we need to be informed, we do
not rely primarily on the press or broadcasting. It is the telephone
which enables us to get messages. Its function is central to our
business world and private life. At the same time a high rating
for word-of-mouth communication can be detected in the way
we choose our doctor or hospital, the shops we visit, the clothes
and furniture we buy, the schools where we send our children.[2]
Thought and knowledge of the world we live in depend on 'information' but we can acquire most of what is necessary for our
current activities only through people who live in the same

surroundings. It is thanks to what they offer us that 'our' universe exists for us at all.

The media bring to our attention characteristics of objects/ events which we normally do not attend to and also situations which we would never know for they are beyond our scope. What chances would there be for a European to imagine anything about life in a remote African district if there were no media? It is true that the written or oral press brings us news that are in many ways extremely different from the knowledge that we would get by a direct contact with an object or a person. However, even if the words are insufficient and the pictures often flickering, the media oblige us to observe circumstances or things we ignored beforehand. Much bad literature has been devoted to explaining that, thanks to the media, which introduce us to individual representations of other people, some charming, a few rather unpleasant, most merely ordinary, our planet has become a single, powerful community, a 'global village'. This is, of course, grossly exaggerated; we are merely offered short glimpses of various facts; information on any given situation is seldom coherent and continuous enough to help us appraise it. But, even if the 'media people' did much better, the 'village' theory would still be wrong since it postulates that 'seeing' is enough to feel involved in a previously unknown situation.

On the other hand, information is all the more accepted and understood if it is related to familiar problems. We are used to stressing the political importance of the newspapers in the eighteenth and nineteenth centuries and it can easily be proved that they played a decisive part in the French Revolution or the development of Chartism. However, if we take into account all the periodicals published during these periods, we see that only a third of them can be classified as 'political'. Some targeted specific professional groups such as merchants or manufacturers. Others were weekly advertisers and their number boomed in provincial cities all through the last century. A third category aimed at local groups (of course mostly at the middle and upper classes) and gave them details about fashion, shopping, the theatre, etc. It is well known that there was an enormous expansion of national newspapers all over Europe after 1960 but what often goes unnoticed is that the local press had boomed long before that so-called 'revolution'. People, in western countries, have been keen on reading newspapers for a long time but they have been searching for information regarding the life of their town or county and have never been primarily interested in political articles, except, of course, during troubled periods such as wartime. Television has won such a huge audience that the permanent influence of the press is generally misunderstood. It is thus necessary to recall that in a good many industrial countries – Britain, Germany, Sweden – the number of people who buy a local newspaper is equal to the number of television viewers.

Contrary to what is often thought, radio, right from the beginning, was far from being only an instrument of unification and centralization. The BBC, for instance, had, between the wars, regional stations which enabled people to talk about themselves, interviewed people and provided information about employment, shopping, roads, religious services and entertainment. The first audience-participation programme was broadcast in 1935 and, from that time onwards, panels of ordinary listeners have been regularly asked to perform in front of or for other listeners who could equally well have been chosen for the panel. After the war, the tendency was accentuated by the creation of ITV which began broadcasting in 1955 in several regions. One of the first weekly talk shows, *Open End*, was so popular that it lasted for nearly thirty years, despite the fact that it had become a bit old-fashioned; its length was undetermined, it went on as long as the debate remained of interest and it took on board tricky questions on sex, immigration and war. It ended in 1984 but, ever since, television and radio have noticeably developed *Crosstalk* in which people discuss problems which interest them. In many countries, viewers/listeners are asked to call and give their opinion or advice which is transmitted live. Many of these people may be individually unreliable but, even if it is not true, what they report is worth broadcasting because listening to it is important to the public. Views or assessments must not be taken at face value; they have a purpose and fulfil a function which is to set up some sort of debate and it is because of this that they are sought and transmitted.

A comparison between the experience of cable television in Belgium and France shows how important the distribution of local information is. Cable television was introduced in both countries at the same time, at the beginning of the 1980s; it was adopted immediately in Belgium whilst it was a failure in France. Despite its promises of instant and constant gratification, cable television was, initially, unable to offer interesting, new programmes. Different though they are, the French television networks are centrally administered which means that cable television could not include topics likely to lure small-town audiences. On the other hand, in Belgium, locally run broadcasting units, relying on largely voluntary contributions and offering infinitely varying programmes dealing with purely local concerns reached a wide variety of viewers: it was the home-shopping network which convinced the Belgians that it was worth paying for cable.

Radio and television talks are basically constructed of separate but intersecting conversations between the interviewees and their host; anyone may intervene if they have in mind to do so. The goal is to achieve a kind of self-sustaining conversation, the host being present to encourage and guide, preventing it from becoming polemical or confused. Andy Warhol proclaimed that 'soon, everyone will be famous for a quarter of an hour'. What he wanted to say was that the media are intent on getting statements or declarations likely to interest their audience, in order to provoke reactions and make the time pass without spending money. Having enjoyed their fifteen minutes, short-lived celebrities allow themselves to go back to a long silence. Up-to-the-minute traffic bulletins, advice on bargain sales or car repairs, instructions in pet care or gardening are what people are happy to transmit to their fellow listeners. Radio and television have contributed to arousing and developing the enjoyment of talking; they have been, at least locally, instruments of sociability. It has often been noted that consumers' relationship with the media is asymmetrical: they are offered information that does not rely on any reciprocal agreement and they may wonder if their attention is not won, in part, by the fact that there is no alternative. As we shall soon see, this is largely true where general information is concerned: people cannot contest or question data communicated by a 'specialist'; they cannot even select them. However, this does not apply to programmes in which the public is asked to intervene.

This is not to say that, by interviewing their clients and becoming, at times, a public sphere, the media help automatically and necessarily to ease social problems. Conflicts arise in restricted areas as well as in larger ones and the fact that people know each other is likely to sharpen or complicate antagonism. In Los Angeles, during the racial unrest of 1992, the local television stations which disclosed police brutality expected that the police might become more careful in order to avoid providing material for the cameras. On the contrary, the police, who were aware of the fact that they could be recognized reacted with even greater violence, beating not only the demonstrators but also the television crews and claiming that television was provoking them in the performance of their duty.

It is not our task, here, to decide whether the media are beneficial or harmful; we are only trying to evaluate their social function. All we can say is that they have persistently reflected decisive changes in social behaviour and that, by recording and exposing them, they have participated in disseminating them. We shall first illustrate what we want to say with two different examples and then try to synthesize our point of view.

Popular magazines, radio and television have been relying more and more, since the middle of the century, on the dissemination of 'neighbourhood stories' (stories dealing with small communities of neighbours. These stories may be fictitious, such as *The Archers*, but they may also be 'real' stories). All of these media make extensive use of series developed over the years, with new stories embodied into the main strand so that they can be extended almost indefinitely; the Americans and Brazilians are the masters of such serials, which sell all over the world. But the 'neighbourhood stories' do not belong in the same category, they do not focus on a family with its domestic hatreds and loves but rather on the relationship between a small group of people and their social environment. *The Archers*, which has been on air since May 1950, may be taken as an archetypal example. The Archers and their friends have been living for years in an invented, paradigmatic village called Ambridge. Nothing 'happens' to them; they are content with coming and going; it is a world of women's institutions, bring-and-buy sales in aid of the parish church and nosy gossips. Unknown protagonists coming out of the blue appear and vanish while the main characters change their mood and habits drastically according to the prevailing fashion, a hard feminist being, for instance, transformed into a dedicated housewife and vice versa. Realism is not what is sought; protagonists worry about their pets' health, indulge in puns and often seem to speak only to pass the time. Although it is difficult to explain why so many listeners have been enjoying this radio series for such a long time, it is not absurd to think that it is its display of humour, sympathy and relaxation which is appreciated.

The same pattern has been adopted by a good many radio

or television series which consist of a clever combination of harm-less jokes with some of the coarseness and closeness generated by a long-lasting familiarity. The media put daily concerns and fictional, but not unbelievable, situations side by side and then, by interrupting the former with adverts and the latter with news, blur the seemingly well-established distinction between the 'genres'. It is no wonder that the one adopts the vocabulary of the other and that fictional characters are taken as being illus-trations of social change or backwardness. This does not happen because readers/viewers/listeners are deceived by their magazines or broadcast programmes, but because, in the very limited field related to talks, chat shows and local events, magazines, radio and television illustrate a way of life familiar to many of their clients and provide some of them with a chance to participate in an active, committed cycle of exchanges.

By asking their customers to participate in their activities, the media tend to obscure the division between the private and public spheres. They urge the interviewees to disclose their pri-vate life and answer intrusive, sometimes lubricious questions. Local radio or television and 'popular' newspapers are often blamed for thinking in headlines and looking mostly for dirt. The success of 'tabloid' newspapers with a relatively small page size and many pictures, has even been interpreted as a symptom of declining political awareness. Again, we are not concerned with either criticizing or praising the tabloid press, we must only wonder about their influence. The intrusion into people's privacy is not something new, it has existed since the beginning of the stamped press. The proliferating cheap newspapers of the mid-nineteenth century were replete with details sometimes poignant, frequently horrific and repulsive about purely domestic affairs. 'Popular' magazines have long been inquiring into the life of stars of sport and screen, politicians and royal families and have disclosed as much scandal as is possible without risking being sued. However, all they have done is to transfer on to well-known individuals what has been currently experienced by more ordinary people. Bourgeoise societies of the late nineteenth century were intent on diffusing a positive image of the nuclear family; for that reason, the press was filled with family celebrations, the home activities of 'the great' provided edifying examples of household unity; their births, marriages and deaths were transformed into family ceremonies, public events interfered with the intimacy of private life. In the twentieth century the cohesion of the group has begun to look less important than personal happiness and has no longer been corroborated by ritual. Cinema was the first to explore new relationships between genders and generations; it did not suppress families but portrayed them as open to external influences and unable to sustain a stable association of their members. Films, which attract limited audiences, were probably ahead of their time whereas the other media have simply been reverberating changes in the most accepted image of kinship and sexual intercourse. It is true that the press has contributed in emphasizing this evolution. But, by disclosing affairs in which sportsmen and women or politicians are involved, the media simply make it clear that an irreproachable home life is not what most people are seeking.

Beyond local horizons

Tabloids are criticized because they print sensational stories about the sexual affairs of stars or royalty. There is nothing original in their practices. It must be remembered that more excitement has always been generated by stories of the life and death of the rich and powerful than by revelations about ordinary citizens, so much so that, by focusing on the upper class, the media simply try to fulfil the expectations of their clients. In the last century, they echoed the moral discourse of the time when they portrayed the impeccable private behaviour of actors or statesmen and they are in tune with another period when they show that, with regard to their personal life, the same sort of people want to be free of any moral allegiance.

The example of stars or politicians is noteworthy because it shows how difficult it is to define the boundaries of what can be talked about in the mass media. Weekly newspapers or local magazines rightly care about the health of those who live in their district but why do the media comment upon the health of foreign statesmen? And why is it that so many people care about it? Why are people so intent on getting news about situations which are miles away from their daily lives? Durkheim has developed a dual model based on the opposition between what he called a 'primitive' and a 'differentiated' society which can help us understand why as much information as possible may be absolutely necessary. Durkheim knew that it was impossible to find any example of a very simple social organization but he built one up for a theoretical purpose. In a small, isolated group, everyone would be placed in the same conditions of existence, would share the same characteristics and would be related to the same people, animals and objects. Consequently, everyone would participate in the same limited knowledge of an immediate environment. Contrasting with this purely conceptual model, highly differentiated societies are, Durkheim assumed, much more complicated; They are divided into specialized spheres so that what their members have to comprehend in order to survive, shifts from the local and concrete to the general and abstract.[3] The loss of primal connection with nature has endowed the city dwellers with a deep sensitivity to the external world and an awareness of the necessity to learn what is going beyond their limited horizon. To begin with, in industrial societies, getting the latest information on the progress of technology is vital. At the same time, the connections between national economies are so multiple that changes in a single country are likely to affect other areas: the physical condition of a few important managers or politicians may influence the Stock Exchange and cause fluctuations in share prices.

Durkheim is right when he emphasizes the usefulness of information in diversified economies. However, even in 'primitive' communities, for instance, in small, out-of-the-way villages of the medieval period, we can detect a curiosity for what was happening outside. Most villagers had imprecise notions about the external world but they were keen on getting 'news' from the few travellers who crossed their path. It is because human beings are generally interested in what does not concern them directly that we have inherited many a treatise about the customs, history and institutions of ancient civilizations.

Whatever its cultural origins are, there has been a perennial need, among societies, to capture something of what is occurring in the world. From an explanatory point of view, there is very little that can be said either about the origins of this interest or about its mode of operation. If curiosity is a recurrent feature of human behaviour, the seeming ubiquity granted by the printed press and other media has profoundly modified the relationship of people to the outside world. Before the middle of the eighteenth century orally transmitted stories about past ages, especially about wars, epidemics and great catastrophes, were the staples of most community lore. The creation of a new means of information was not a simple step forward, but a broadening of what could be apprehended previously. The press and then broadcasting introduced first, a multiplicity of horizons; even the rudimentary magazines of the eighteenth century described different places. Media information has long hinted at dual polarities, here/else-where, us/them; it is not pure data but entails a conception of the world as a simultaneity of various actions and situations. There is also the style of media – their language is not merely descriptive but rather connects various facts to each other, thus giving the impression that they provide a guide not simply to passive acceptance but to an active understanding of the world. Another important feature of the media is their presentation; Elisabeth Bowen nicely evokes the newspapers full of 'photographs of statesmen and battleships, scantily clad girls, sports cars and oaked-beamed rooms, of funny stories and pictures'.[4] However critical it sounds, her list conveys the impression of variety produced by a quick look at any medium. We are accustomed nowadays to think of 'information' (or entertainment as will be seen later) as being what is first expected from the media. Yet some of our mental activity is composed of visual, oral and tactile reactions and our response to the news is largely dependent on the aspect of the media. The arrangement of material (for instance, the position of headlines, the nature of visual images) predetermines for us certain modes of observation and interpretation so that, when studying a medium, sociologists must learn to resist the temptation to place greater emphasis on what it 'says' and pay attention to what it looks like.

Most of the time, the media transcend our daily reality while maintaining a close connection to problems associated with our daily concerns. They tell us about people or regions which do not belong to our immediate surroundings but are likely to modify our situation. What is reported fulfils our longing for more news and may turn out to be useful or at least instructive. This explains why the 'content' of media has been, for a long time, a major topic for debate, some commentators charging the 'popular' media with making money from the public's abiding taste for scandal and the macabre, others emphasizing the value, in our world, of precise, up-to-date information. Both are right. From a moralist's position the media are decidedly ambivalent instruments. But, if we consider them in the light of Weber's scheme, they appear to be rational tools which help people understand their time and satisfy their eagerness to observe other people.

Mass media are often charged with altering or even inventing dramatic situations and a good deal of empirical material confirms that opinion. Let us consider two different examples likely to throw light on this. In the summer and autumn of 1888, six women were killed and mutilated in London's East End. Contemporaries, struck by the similarity between the crimes, attributed them to a unique murderer whose nickname, Jack the Ripper, played a large part in establishing the supposed identity of the criminal. It seems that the letter signed 'Jack the Ripper' which was sent to the central news agency after the second murder was forged by a journalist. A century later the whole world was shaken when television showed pictures of opponents slaughtered by the Rumanian police at Timisoara and the indignation with the massacre hastened the fall of the communist government. After a few days it was disclosed that the pictures were a fraud: the filmmakers had photographed corpses taken from a nearby hospital and made the scene more gripping by using simulated gunfire. Diverse though they are, both these instances show how the media can contribute to creating a legend and developing a climate of terror. It is clear that the Londoners believed that Jack the Ripper existed since his signature was in the daily newspapers. Those who saw the Rumanian corpses on their television set, that is to say almost on location, were sure that these were political victims. However, if we can assume that people are easily fooled, we are unable to point to the mechanism at work here. Was it only because it was printed or filmed that the public accepted the version contrived by the media? Or was it that, by focusing on one fact (a man, a slaughter) newspapers or television forced their patrons to see the circumstances in a different light and switch from feeling a vague concern to more precise feelings – fear in London, wrath about Rumania. That people reacted to the news is a fact not easily explained and a good deal of research is needed to find out the reasons why, in different circumstances, opinion is disposed to accept or treat lightly what it is told by the media.

Audience surveys reveal connections between regular reading of the tabloids or avid television viewing and the expression of a lasting worry about street violence and a permanent fear of aggression. Since 'popular' means of information emphasize crime, what could be inferred from the above-mentioned relationship? A quick answer is that sensational reporting and excessive coverage of bloodshed create a long-lasting state of anxiety. But it could also be said that angst-ridden people look for periodicals in which they will find sanguine stories or, in a less conclusive way, that media consumption and personal involvement share certain common roots.

Events

Let us look again at the Rumanian example, the so-called Timisoara slaughter. That was not the first time that demonstrators had been killed by guns in a communist country; cinema and television had previously documented the repression in Hungary or Czechoslovakia without giving rise to such excitement. We are not concerned, here, with explaining why the Rumanian affair, which was an episode in the final crisis of the communist bloc, roused worldwide indignation. All we want to stress is that incidents which happen in different locations, however similar they are, are perceived in extremely contrasting ways.

What makes the difference between the facts that we remark upon and those that we ignore? Is news something which makes itself noticeable and which mass media simply report? News does not arrive spontaneously onto the desk of editors, it has to be collected, disseminated by news agencies and reshaped and refined by journalists for more general circulation. It is therefore the manner in which a fact is reported which sets it apart from similar facts which pass unnoticed. Mass media have been used for many years to organize news items into transmittable items, told in a succinct, unfolding form and given a structure which identifies them as being of importance. The media have thus the enormous power of defining news and the next chapter will examine how this is the foundation of their influence and prosperity but, first, we shall focus on the relationship between the 'news' and those who report it.

Let us start from a simpler situation: local informers tell a news agency, or a newspaper, that 'something' has happened. An event that has been lived abruptly, sometimes incoherently, by direct witnesses has to be reconstructed as a coherent fact. Details are obtained by going to official spokesmen, especially the police but also local authorities, associations, pressure groups and, finally, individuals who validate the data. The possible sources are limited, which explains why the same news stories can be read in most newspapers or heard on most broadcast programmes. It is not our task, here, to analyse the strategies of the various possible sources of information but we cannot help noticing how critical these strategies are for the 'creation' of the news.

The accuracy of information depends originally on the policy and aims of the news sources. In many instances actors, for example the police, are taken between the fear of leaking too many details and the necessity to demonstrate that they are very effective. However, things are not simple and unilateral. Popular access to information and knowledge is held to be a fundamental democratic right and even totalitarian governments boast about telling their fellow citizens 'what is really happening'. Informing may be a way of directing public opinion. Take the case of terrorism. It is tempting to take away doubts or fears by minimizing the effects of bomb attacks or kidnappings. It is also admitted that terrorists depend on the media for publicity. But emphasizing the threat is likely to make people accept strong repression which, otherwise, would be criticized.[5] There is a permanent interrelation between the inquisitiveness of the media, the institutions that they report and the expectations of the public. A good example is provided by election campaigns which, for a long time, have been essentially what is communicated by the means of information: candidates cannot eschew the questions of journalists; it is even vital for them to be interviewed and have their name in the newspapers or their face on the television screen. On the pretext of avoiding the pressures of public opinion, MPs were long reluctant to have their proceedings publicized. They also knew that there was no other way out and that by making their work more accountable to the electors they would improve their image. For that reason parts of parliamentary debates are broadcast all over the world. Media coverage may help overcome awkward situations, a face-to-face on television can be effective with a controversial subject and a good interviewer and is, at any rate, likely to draw huge audiences, which is a kind of advertisement.

Any fact reported by a medium is a reconstruction, the coherence of which is furnished by recourse to existing models of storytelling. Those who have taken part in the event, those who have witnessed it or those who have the right to disseminate official information about it are all keen on establishing their version of the facts. Once their account has been widely disseminated, once it has been printed and shown on television, it acquires some sort of obviousness; it becomes the standard rendering of the event. Reporters, who have first to collect data and then to pass them on to their medium, occupy, therefore, a rather ambiguous position in the circulation of news. In their relationship with their informants, they find themselves simultaneously buoyed up by mutual trust and locked into mutually reinforced distrust. While the journalists ponder the reliability of those who tell them a story, the latter consider the chance of being misunderstood or betrayed by the former. The production of news is a complex operation but we can consider three typical situations.

First, in some circumstances, journalists are given by their informant a ready-made communiqué that they cannot modify. It is what happens during wars when governments manipulate the news for their own purposes. It is the case, as well, with totalitarian regimes which determine that the public is not aware and must not become aware of what is going on for if they did, they would not support it. Even in peace time and in liberal systems many bodies, public or private, are eager to impose their truth on the media. The hesitancy or silence of corporations which do not want to disclose their losses result in an obsessive accumulation of detail which has no other purpose than to create an impression of seriousness and compensate for a lack of precise data.

Second, the media can also challenge the official account, underline its inconsistencies and disclose hidden facts. During the last years of the American intervention in Vietnam both the press and television played a decisive part in exposing what the policy of the White House was. The official truth was that the United States was withdrawing from Southeast Asia. But, by mid-1969, the *New York Times* printed reports which contradicted the accredited statements and revealed that the US Air-Force had been ordered to bomb Cambodia, a neutral country. Then television took over from the newspapers and illustrated, day after day, dramatic or unpleasant aspects of the American presence in Vietnam. The right-wing magazines tried to offer their readers a more reassuring interpretation, opening thus a violent struggle between supporters and opponents of the government line. Until the end of the war (January 1973) the battle for news was a key element in the political evolution of the United States.[6]

Finally, the media may also expand on details which passed first unnoticed and create an event out of bits of seemingly negligible information. The best known case is the intervention of the *Washington Post* in the Watergate Affair. In June 1972, intruders were caught in Democratic Party Headquarters. The *Post*, backed by the *New York Times*, began an inquiry which transformed a trite episode of burglary into a political case. Radio and television were soon involved in a harsh controversy which resulted in President Richard Nixon's impeachment and resignation (August 1974).

Superficial though it is, this short list shows that the enunciation of an event is the final stage of a complicated transaction.[7] If we want to understand this process we have to scrutinize both the strategy of the pressure groups, institutions and big corporations towards the media and the informational policy of the media themselves: the relationship between the former and the latter is indeed a difficult one. It is not even necessary to make the emphasis switch from straight reporting to interpretation and debate; a mere statement such as 'Cambodia has been bombed by US aircraft' can be crucial in the evolution of public attitude. Informants and media mongers are therefore obliged to check very carefully what they can or what they want to publicize.

Deciding to diffuse or conceal news is all the more problematic as the response of audiences is not easily predictable. When 'something' happens the influence of the media certainly increases in size. The Watergate hearings, led by the American Congress at the beginning of 1973 forced the national newspapers to augment their print runs. Television watching expanded significantly, radio and television networks were obliged to split to provide extra coverage; hearings were also repeated early in the morning and late at night. In this respect it can be said that the operation was a success.[8] However it would be misleading to accept the figures at face value. Those who bought a newspaper day after day or spent their night watching their screen did not belong to the regular audience. Arguing that the timetable was upset and that the ordinary target audiences were no longer reading or watching, the advertising companies decided to stop part of their campaigns which resulted in the shrinking of advertising revenue. What is more, after an initial burst of enthusiasm, people began to tire. Some of the witnesses were moving or funny but, despite interesting individual performances, the physical presence of many interlocutors was colourless and most of the coverage was visually uninteresting; nothing could distract the viewers' attention from what was being said, which was not necessarily exciting. Yet, it is difficult to know what to make of this evidence, for the broadcasting of the hearings made a great impact on the American public. One year after Nixon had resigned, a sample of interviewed Americans remembered the key themes developed by the witnesses and sometimes the exact terms that they had used. Most of those who participated in this later interview believed that they had spent much time watching television during the crisis, but it was not clear whether what they explained was what they had seen or what friends had told them. It seems that the hearings were widely commented upon and that the public was informed by word of mouth as much as by direct attention to the reports of the media.

Unexpected, shocking events attract immediate interest. Most Americans understood, almost on the first day of the *Post*'s campaign, that the 'burglary' at the Democratic Headquarters was not a banal affair. Despite the press coverage of the case, the television reporting was very discrete. This difference can be easily explained. The newspapers, which accused the Republican administration of spying on its adversaries addressed a public that was mostly hostile to Nixon's policy and highly concerned with political issues. The television networks turned to a much larger audience; they selected topics that were general and imprecise enough so as to appeal to any type of viewer without displeasing any of them. When it appeared that the interest of the public was not decreasing, radio and television gave more and more coverage to the Watergate Affair. Undoubtedly the media attempt to maintain their share of the market against rivals. But the development of the Watergate Affair shows that their desire to gratify their respective publics is not always in tune with the latter's expectations and that, sometimes, they are obliged to follow their clientele rather than orientate it.

Informing the public about 'events' is not a simple task. Dramatic episodes such a plane crash in which important politicians are killed can make a great impression, increase the circulation of newspapers and make viewers stay longer in front of their television set. But how long do strong feelings last? There is no answer to the question. The Falklands War and Gulf War were widely covered by the media; the production of news in these distant countries demanded a considerable deployment of resources. But, in both cases, the main events occurred over a limited period of time, the audiences' interest was short-lived and the expenditure involved was not compensated for by intensifying the influence of newspapers or broadcasting on their customers. It is only in the long term that the relationship between the general public and a fact, or a series of facts, can be evaluated. This is the reason why we must refer to the Vietnam War, which lasted for nearly three decades and was the major international news story of the twentieth century.

After the end of the Vietnam War it was often said that the Vietnamese had won, not through their military achievement, but as the consequence of the war's portrayal by the American media. Actually, the factual information found in newspapers or broadcasts was limited and rather unsubstantial, at least until the end of the 1960s. Official pressure was exerted upon the journalists, but the White House, whose aims were indecisive, was mostly keen on avoiding public disquiet about the costs of operations and did not advertise its policy. In February 1968 the picture, and then the film, of a South Vietnamese officer executing a Viet Cong terrorist in a street in Saigon evoked a strong emotional reaction. However, this was an exception; the media tended to minimize casualties and to show mostly pictures of accurate air strikes. At times, the war seemed no longer to be news of the day and for a few days it was not even mentioned. When he arrived at the White House (1969) Richard Nixon announced that the United States were on their way out of Vietnam, but it took America four more years to get out of the war. During this final stage, Vietnam was recurrently present in the media. At first the issue was presented as a secondary one since the fighting was supposed to come to an end very soon. Then, with the bombing of Cambodia, the Americans realized that hostilities would be prolonged; the initial optimism was substituted with a gravity which indicated to everybody that an honourable end was not at hand. The news then illustrated the vascillation of the government and public opinion which were upset by mounting casualties but did not want to be defeated. In reporting events, the media mostly reflected with relative immediacy the variation in the White House's attitude as well as the American people's awareness of a hopeless situation.

The essential elements during the years 1969–1973, i.e. the incompatibility between two contradictory aims and the awkward position of the media which had to take this lack of consistency into account help us to question the notion of 'event'. What was an event during that period? An exceptional offensive or a routine bombing? What may an episode or a fact actually be when the interest of everybody – informants, news mongers and news consumers – is so labile? Facts could be seen as parts of a system: there was the day when Washington sent 'counsellors' to Saigon, the day the United States openly intervened in the war, etc. But systems, too, evolve over time. The official disembarkment of American troops was no longer an event once it was admitted that America had been interfering long before that day. This is a typical change in impact; what was initially of paramount import-ance becomes a mere detail which, nevertheless, might be of great significance in another system, for instance in a survey of the lies coming from the White House during the war.

Mass media sell news. However, the definition of news items depends first, upon a bargain between information sources and journalists, then, upon the ways facts are formulated and even-tually upon the organization of understanding on the part of the public. The notion of war, for instance, depends not upon a series of bombings and attacks but upon how such episodes are presented and related to one another during the three aforemen-tioned stages. But is it the content of information which matters? Since the printed press began to develop very rapidly, that is to say since the middle of the eighteenth century, millions of people have been informed about more events in a single week than they would once have been able to see in a year or even in the course of a lifetime. It is not only a question of quantity but of variety as well; magazines or broadcasts seldom concentrate on a unique topic – they mix up trivia and drama, elaborate docu-mentaries and hastily made reportage, recorded interviews and live talks. Variety induces inattention. It also broadens people's horizons. But nobody can tell whether the permanent supply of new details erases the old ones or helps to understand them better: this is a question of lived experience which is beyond social sciences' capacity of analysis.

Grand occasions

The media tell us about aspects of what is occurring in the world. They also participate in special events by broadcasting them and announcing them well in advance which stimulates public interest because they have been so widely publicized that it is impossible not to have heard of them. Grand occasions of that sort are not something new. In the past, people used to pay tribute to their sovereigns and leaders. In each locality, religious ceremonies and speeches marked the birth, coronation, wedding and death of the monarch. There were special days commemorating wars, especially in the nineteenth century, after the long ordeal of the Napoleonic wars. In the then divided Germany, battle survivors stood at gravesides and honoured the memory of those who had given their life to defend German soil. Festivities were symbolic events, organized around an interpretation of the past, or around a personality. Counties, cities and villages developed historical images of that kind to fit political and social needs. Events of public interest were not only celebrated, they were also a pretext for performances in theatres. The coronation of George IV in Westminster Abbey (1821) was restaged at Drury Lane as were many other ceremonies throughout the nineteenth century.

As the circulation and impact of the press grew, national and local leaders used it to herald public ceremonies while the newspapers found in commemorations a pretext for publishing non-controversial articles. However, it is the audiovisual media which changed the situation by providing an entire country with the same account at more or less the same time. At the beginning of the twentieth century, written chronicles were displaced by pictures which focused on the physical presence of the 'great' and helped shore up the political unity of each country. Radio was even more powerful, it transformed public celebrations into performances for simultaneous consumption and enabled the progression of a procession to be followed, step by step. Television has introduced a supplementary touch of immediacy but the main transformation had occurred earlier, when listeners to radio had been given the chance to use their imagination and take part in collective celebrations.

Events can be unimportant, that is to say, they will not change our situation in any way. Their significance resides in the fact that they are ritualized and that the media stress their historicity. As Daniel Dayan and Elihu Katz put it, the commitment of media 'is definitional. It recognizes the event, conveys its distinctive features and exposes its constitutive rules.'[9] Unlike ordinary daily events, grand occasions are publicized well in advance. Expectation contributes to mark them out. For months prior to the chosen day, all those who will take part are engaged in preparations in order to meet the expectations of the public which, for its part, requires information about the progress of rehearsals.

The broadcasting of a grand occasion can be characterized by three dominant features: it is live, it is not interrupted, it is received by millions of people. This sounds extremely simplified, but in fact the combination of these features makes it difficult to analyse what people intend to do when following this kind of transmission. Every viewer is aware of participating in some sort of gigantic operation. All those who watch, or listen, are members of a 'communality' (to borrow Weber's expression), that is to say, of an ephemeral group of people brought together by a fleeting curiosity. The conviction that they share in a collective activity is so strong that viewers usually gather in one another's homes to watch the television. And, because it is broadcast live, there is only a single moment in which the event can be seen or heard in common. Interested viewers watch with relatives or neighbours instead of watching alone at home. Some researchers go so far as to believe that such events, which are advertised far in advance, break daily routine and stress consensual values, thus triggering feelings of collective participation and a sharing of concerns. However, except in particular circumstances such as the Kennedy funeral, it seems that the readers/viewers can simultaneously pay special attention to the account of such an event and also be very critical about the occurrence or about the way it is presented. What matters is that such an occasion provokes various forms of interaction. Since it is announced in advance, people know that it will be reported and it will provide a topic for conversation or debates. People gather together for different reasons (involvement, criticism, or the simple pleasure of being together), forming thus an ephemeral sociation.

A survey such as the one we have just mentioned should make us think about the definition of media content. Nobody would sustain the idea that broadcast programmes or newspapers give an objective picture of the world. It is widely acknowledged that cameras distort reality by framing their subject and modifying the distances between people or things. The words used have no fixed meaning, interacting and leaving the text signifying something different from what it was supposed to say. Also, any news item is placed in a certain order and this and the length of time devoted to it fixes its importance in the overall sequence of news items which make up a magazine or a news bulletin. It is the relation a certain item has with other news items that we view as 'news of the day'. The formative influence of the media is not limited to the creation of news; it also influences our perception of news. But the readers/viewers are not passive consumers; they are used to skimming through the pages of their newspapers or to channel hopping so that the items assembled into a larger whole may be detached and reassembled by any user into different wholes.

The 'content' of the media can be analysed in two different

ways. It is first, what the media do when they select certain facts, dissociate them from their original context and reinsert them in a world of news. For that reason we have tried to understand how those who work in the media are informed and how they produce what they call information. The content is also what the clients absorb. We cannot deduce either from the text or discussions or from the pictures what will be understood. At best, we can make assumptions about possible interpretations and plausible connections. Content must be seen both in its own right and as part of a process. However, explaining how millions of users react in different, specific situations is not feasible. We have therefore attempted to study the context in which people use the media in a wider manner. This context is not the particular position in which each individual receives the news but rather the expectations of the consumers and also the needs which might be fulfilled by information. We have delineated three broad situations which are not empirically defined but designate three types of relationship. A first case is the community taken as a spatially delimited social system: information provided by local media has a significant part in maintaining links between people living in the same surroundings. It is used as a tool by the members of a preexisting group. Second, on a larger scale, where the relationship becomes impersonal and is regulated by defined, precise aims, for instance a large city, or a nation, information is a frame of reference. We shall come back, at the end of the chapter, to the cohesive function of the media in the modern world but we have already shown that the media help people to make sense of the world in which they live and that they satisfy a desire to observe other people. Information is used by individuals to define, in extremely different ways, their relationship to others. Eventually, and this is the third case, the account of a few, well publicized events gives people an opportunity to gather together and form a transient sociation; in this case the content of the report is the pretext of an interaction between individuals.

RELAXATION

Most of the time, media studies deal with information as it is collected, elaborated and disseminated by the press and broadcasting media. From a political point of view, it is crucial to analyse the media, to evaluate their reliability and to denounce the bias that they introduce in their presentation of events. But the great majority of the media are not merely concerned with current affairs or international issues; many of them are more intent on providing their customers with entertainment than with news and serious, topical comment. It is true that distinguishing between information and entertainment is sometimes very difficult. The media have for years been disseminating a great deal of scientific knowledge although in simplified form; they have also stirred the imagination about the mysteries of the animal world of people whose interest is usually more excited by sensational pictures than by scientific inquiry. Is a docudrama restaging a recent international crisis instructive or purely recreative? How shall we classify an ethnographic documentary which narrates how a primitive tribe has been affected by industrial pollution? One possible answer is that it is the public which decides how it will receive and interpret an article or a programme, but individual choices are beyond our reach. Mentioning them is a mere formality which does not allow us to understand how the diverting part of the media can be treated by sociologists. It is this problem that we should now examine.

Pleasure

An important, perfectly obvious difference between information and entertainment is the manner in which the public is being addressed. A news item or report is written or presented by someone – a journalist, an announcer, a panel of specialists – who stress and explain a series of facts. This implies that, in informative documentaries, the pictures are often complementary and merely help to convey a text which is making the argument. 'Serious' newspapers, in Europe or America, avoided photographs as long as they could. In films or on television the commentator explains with authority while the image creates a mood and suggests a context in which the relevant topic is placed naturally. Without this voice, radio or television programmes would have difficulty in coping with abstract scientific or political debates but, as soon as there is an explanatory comment, listeners/viewers are told something. On the other hand, there is little, if anything, to be learnt from entertainment programmes and, from that point of view, it can be said that the media offer a diversion in the original sense of this word: something which causes us to change direction, which distracts our attention. From what? This is an important question and we shall see how Marxism tries to answer it. Let us assume, for the time being, that it diverts us from serious issues. To a large extent, the use of the media is inspired by the matrix of pleasure and desire. Audiences cannot be seen as millions of ears and eyes absorbing attentively what they are offered. Not only do they evaluate and criticize, but they intervene more actively by taking physical pleasure as with heavy metal rock bands, playing video games or watching wrestling. People want music to dance to, they want television programmes to fit in with home life and films to suit children in the school holiday. In other words they have a functional conception of the media, which means that if they can neither modify nor improve the programmes, they are able to use them for their own needs. In some circumstances, they even manage to obtain what the media mongers would much prefer not to give them. That is what happened with the success of rock and roll: in the 1950s the radio networks which had stored a large amount of light music or jazz and wanted to make it pay were unable to resist the growing infatuation for blues singers.

Gauging the amount of pleasure people take in consuming the media is of course impossible. But we can try to comprehend some of its origins. Habit plays its part in the loyalty of audiences, as we have observed when speaking of routines. Recurrence, which enables one to plan one's own recreation is highly appreciated. Media producers often complain about their public's reluctance to accept changes. When a magazine modifies its format, when radio or television schedule their quizzes, game shows or sporting events at a different time, the bulk of the audience is generally strongly opposed to the change so that new schedules have to be announced much in advance to avoid protests. However, routine must not be interpreted as an obedient absorption of standardized messages. Although we lack empirical evidence, for very little research has been carried out in this field, it seems that people are more capable of putting media productions to unpredictable and highly personal uses when they are very familiar with them and have been using them over a long period of time.

Examples are provided by two different cases – games and porno magazines or films. Unlike gambling, games in the tabloid newspapers, quizzes and other competitions on radio and television are not a predominantly male, adult pursuit. The difference lies neither in the rules nor in the prospects for all these schemes seem to be governed by chance. But the rituals are significantly unalike. There is no need to stake money, no necessity to go to a special place to take part in the games so that housewives or children can compete. It is a system which requires some shrewdness and is better played collectively; radio or television often have teams taking part and individual challengers like to have friendly supporters when they are invited to compete in a studio. These games bring a person celebrity status rather than money. They make a person famous for fifteen minutes, in front of his/her friends. A uniform, periodic unfolding of events is therefore basic to the ceremonial. Contenders-to-be watch regularly and carefully, they know the rules and do not want anything to be modified.

The case of pornography has nothing to do with games. It is mentioned here because the pictures used in porno films or magazines are incredibly repetitive – to such an extent that the same shots are often recycled in several movies. Formulaic though they are, porno productions are neither straight representations of some act, nor incitements to do whatever they represent. What counts is that they differ from other narratives in being structured by sexual drive with alternating foreplay and climax. The response porno products elicit is based upon recurrent combinations of a limited set of sounds and images. This would be rather marginal if pornography was an isolated sector ignored by most media. But sexuality has long been exploited by most media, be it only embodied in crime, divorce, news in brief or adverts. A light, unvaried touch of pornography is to be found in certain tabloid newspapers, magazines, films, songs and, more and more, television programmes. For example, a woman's breast is depicted at the bottom of the financial page of a newspaper; it has no defined significance, no connection with the rest of the page, it is simply there. Semioticians call it an open signifier that people can ignore or interpret in contrasting ways.

Competence

There is a creative side in any form of reception so that the experience and competence of the public, what we might call its media culture, has also to be taken into account. Deciphering the intended meaning or message conveyed by a paper or a poster implies some skill. The users have to learn the system of signs which, by social conventions, stand for a particular object or circumstance. The content of a newspaper article cannot be reduced to the substance of the words it contains. Its title, length, print and make-up are to be considered; it is up to the reader to pay attention to the conventions embodied in the pattern of a periodical. In audiovisual productions cinematic types of expression are interrelated to form a logical system of 'language'. Viewers must take notice of the particular framing of a character, of the variations in scale, of the panning of the camera and tracking shots if they want to make sense of the story. However, films, unlike written texts, do not have a strict grammar which determines how camera angles, lighting and distances are to be incorporated into larger units. The content of each film shot has many signifiers and is virtually an assertion or sentence in itself so that viewers are permanently required to interpret what they see. Analysing the audience who watch television soaps, a 'genre' that is particularly repetitive and unvaried, Christine Geraghty has shown[10] that women are extremely sensitive to what she calls a 'sense of excess', that is to say a permanent mixing up of different styles and references. The women interviewed after watching the soaps distance themselves from the story even when they confess that they have been gripped. They are able to understand the conventions of the genre, they laugh at their crudity and they underline the surrealistic features of American family life as it is featured in popular serials. The most noticeable point in the research is that the viewers are fond of soaps, are keen on watching them regularly but consider them cheap, poor, hastily made entertainment.

Commercial propaganda is possibly the sector where an attentive, creative audience is most needed. Adverts frequently presuppose a certain sophistication in their audience. This was not necessarily the case at the outset of the present century when publicity attempted at convincing potential customers that a given good was the best and most efficient in its field. In the mid-1920s a broadcast advert for Pepsodent toothpaste said: 'Modern scientists demand science; they believe nothing else. The scientists in the Pepsodent toothpaste laboratories have proved certain facts. They know that Pepsodent removes dangerous films off teeth . . .', etc. One of the major aims of advertisements over the years has been to persuade. However, instead of informing, advertising has also attempted to entertain. This strategy is based upon a different reaction: if the readers or viewers have experienced a moment of pleasure they will associate it with the brand and, remembering this when they see the product, they will be tempted to buy it. Advertising is fairly different from pure information when it becomes a miniature quiz and teases the viewer: 'Are you clever enough to guess what this is or what that means?' Industrial companies noticed this from the beginning of the nineteenth century onwards. Some of them, especially soap producers[11] bought the copyrights of famous paintings or drawings and printed them on wrappings or on posters. Sometimes they made small changes to introduce the goods they wanted to advertise: when it was detected, it made the consumer feel very clever and more willing to buy the product.

However, the periodicals were unable to take advantage of emotions which the broadcast media are likely to manipulate. For radio and television have resources denied to the press: they take advantage of the unfolding of time by rapidly developing the sequence 'question/pause/answer' and by solving the problem at virtually the same moment that they pose it. Advertising which attempts to seduce gives no information and tells a story without it being obvious which product is being advertised. Consider a cinema/television advert. While massaging a client, a masseuse asks another lady whether 'it Voooh? – Vzzzz? – Rmmm?'; she illustrates what she means by energetically slapping, clapping and kneading the back of her client. We cannot help wondering what she is talking about. The answer is provided in the last shot showing an electric food-mixer which makes the sounds, 'Voooh – Vzzzz – Rmmm'. The film leaves a twenty-second gap which the viewer will perhaps try to fill by an analogy which comes not from the advertiser but from the receiver. Many adverts are made by resorting to the insight of the viewers in a way which seems to run against the grain of their explicit purpose. The futuristic machines and exotic landscapes displayed on the screen are likely to mislead those who have not understood that the world of publicity is not the world in which they live and that their car will not take off and land in a tropical island as some vehicles do in publicity films. Advertisers have not changed their aim, they still want to lure potential buyers but, instead of telling them what they need to understand, they try to please them. Solid, practical goods have been metamorphosed into riddles, the key ingredient (apart from good filming and editing) being irony. Even announcements are aimed at a competent public.[12]

The making of entertainment

Information is best characterized by newness and didactism. On the other hand, recurrence and fantasy are typical of entertainment. In the realm of entertainment, the media offer a limited variety of genres. The word 'genre' is surely inappropriate and could be substituted by 'kind', or 'type', but because it is a familiar word, we shall use it, here, in a very loose sense. A genre is not a well-defined category, rather it is a label that people give to works akin to each other. Representatives of a genre can make up a group whose elements are related in various ways without necessarily having specific features in common. Westerns, which constitute one of the less arguable genres, do not always take place in the American West; some have no sheriff, no horses and no cowboys. The notion of a genre may be defined by the fact that it is a convention: after some time the readers or viewers get used to thinking of a 'western' or a 'talk show', or 'docudrama' as a certain kind of product.[13] Genres cannot be regarded as given entities. They are not even the outcome of a purely internal evolution of media production. A long, and sometimes very conflicting process decides which of a series of possible options will actually be implemented. It is necessary to illustrate this complex process by looking at two different cases – the development of different genres in cinema and the evolution of broadcast music.

In its golden age, Hollywood popularized two emblematic figures, the tall, handsome cowboy, conqueror of the American West and the punchy, energetic 'city boy',[14] alternately gangster and FBI agent. We shall return to the gangster fiction when discussing ideology but the Western deserves a short mention. It was not inevitable that the various movies depicting the American West should have become a genre. Traditionally, the history of the Western can be traced back to the prehistory of the cinema and linked to the stories of cowboys and horse thieves printed in the pulps and dime novels. But up until the middle of the 1920s, the word 'Western' was mostly used as an adjective to describe short (less than an hour), bad-quality films shown in downtown picture halls. The Western during the first three decades of cinema was not a genre because it could not be viewed in isolation. It was shown within a group of different shows or public entertainments and its development cannot be understood properly unless it is related to other forms of entertainment such as the circus, slapstick, comedy and even rodeos. At the end of the 1920s these undefinable, inconsistent forms of entertainment gave birth to the classical Western. The change was attributable to a combination of interests and demands. With the arrival of talking pictures, film studios had to hire scriptwriters to produce elaborate texts instead of hastily made plots. Young, ambitious actors like Gary Cooper were not willing to gesticulate frantically in front of the camera as Tom Mix used to do. They demanded to play complex, intricate roles. While bargaining with their staff, the film studios had to compete with radio which had started to broadcast very popular Western stories such as the adventures of the Lone Ranger broadcast over more than two decades (1933–1954). An America demoralized by the Great Depression wanted both hope and easily defeated enemies. The Westerns were imbued with the ideology of the Frontier and they pictured a mythical enemy, the Red Indian. Previously, Indians were shown in the background of a few movies, but they evoked a vanishing past and were never part of the plot. From the early 1930s to the early 1960s Westerns offered well-ordered stories of conquest and war and the plot depicted positive, optimistic heroes. On screen, in books or on television and radio the classic Western was not simply an agreeable distraction, but condensed conflicting interests and gave them a representational form.

Music is seldom dealt with in media studies because it seems to avoid the bias and distortion which make texts or pictures highly problematical. There is obviously an industrial side to the production of music, i.e. the record companies which pay artists and make records fight hard to sell their products but their demands, however strong these may be, do not seem to influence the style of composers or performers. The interaction between the media, musicians and audiences is not easily perceptible but it affects the making of musical programmes. To begin with, it was not common, before the invention of the gramophone record, to talk about music in general terms. Rather, there were several types of music aimed at different audiences. Once shops began to specialize in selling records, the term 'music' was promoted to the abstract. Even so, audiences were rather limited and radio played a crucial part not only in popularizing the idea that music was accessible to everybody but in revealing little known 'genres'. It sometimes seems difficult to understand why, out of the unsettled period which followed the First World War, a byproduct of African musical tradition, namely jazz, surfaced in the United States and then became popular in Europe. It is impossible to understand why without examining first, the development of records, radio and talking pictures on the one hand, of huge audiences on the other and, second, the degree of interaction which developed between them. Small local dance bands which survived by moving from one dance-hall to another were hired by radio networks and quickly became famous. Radio and cinema were not important simply because they shaped jazz and ensured its reputation, they contributed also to legitimate it. There were strong arguments, up until the middle of the century, about what could be broadcast: educated listeners claimed classical music, popular audiences wanted 'nice tunes' and old songs so that jazz which appealed to both, became the middle-of-the-road music on radio. Before radio and cinema, music audiences were limited in size. Jazz benefited from a popularity that was unprecedented in the experience of American and European bands. Its adoption cannot be explained either by its 'modernism' or by focusing on the new methods of broadcasting. It is the interplay between these two trends which led to a radical shift in the culture and leisure habits of western society.

The co-operation of record companies, broadcasting and film studios was also decisive in helping radio to surmount a temporary crisis and in securing for rock and roll, its reputation. At the end of the 1940s it was taken for granted that the number of radio sets, which had dramatically increased during the war, had come to a halt: people were equipped with radios and would merely replace obsolete ones. But the 45 rpm record was launched in 1949. It represented a format likely to reach the elusive teenagers, a group whose spending habits were changeable as their enthusiasm was short. It was also ideal for 'light' programmes, alternating jocular conversation with music. Thanks to the 45 rpm record, the record-producing companies widened their audience. The radio networks were obliged to follow, and the introduction of transistor radios[15] stimulated the sales of radios. Rock and roll, which might have been a passing fancy, became a fashion. In the middle of the 1960s it was already a relevant musical form, which provided jingles for advertisements. Film and television studios were also keen on substituting it for the symphonic compositions which, previously, had been the theme music of most films. Thanks to plagiarism by advertising, many small bands whose work would otherwise have remained unknown to the general public provided a musical repertoire which became soon familiar to everybody. Backed by radio and television, popularized by

adverts, rock and roll was strong enough to survive technological
changes such as the advent of the long-playing record and to give
birth to an autonomous 'genre', the 'rock music video' or 'pop
video' which in turn, was the basis for music television stations.

The video boom began in 1983 with Michael Jackson's *Thril-
ler*. It happened mostly because the video was broadcast by
America's MTV, the first musical television station. MTV had
made its debut in 1981. It was then impossible to receive it in
Los Angeles or New York and it lost money so that nobody
believed it could survive. A few years later it thrived in the
audiovisual market place, its twenty-four-hour programmes were
transmitted to more than forty countries and subsidiaries had
been established in Europe and Asia. The success was not haphazard, it had been cleverly planned. Combining commercials
based on rock and roll rhythms with promotional shorts for various record companies, MTV was the first television channel that
fulfilled the expectations of the three generations which, since
the middle of the century, had become familiar with rock and
roll and enjoyed it. It is true that, at the outset, the companies
gave their records freely, to have them advertised but, after a
while, they asked for payment. By then, MTV was powerful
enough to afford records and videos because it was able to offer
large audiences to companies selling consumer goods. MTV
adapted successfully to a fluctuating market because it met the
needs of both the record industries and various generations of
the public alike. Thanks to radio and television and backed by
commerce and advertising, a few musical styles – jazz, swing, rock
and roll and pop – have so deeply penetrated audiences' habits
that they embody the tastes of the twentieth century.

Contrasting information and relaxation at the beginning of
this section, we said that the former is fluctuating and didactic,
the latter repetitive and escapist. We must now complete our
initial statement. It is in the media themselves that information
finds its origin and its main reference: an event is simply a fact
selected for the media and reported and commented on by them.
The only thing people can do to understand it better or to get
more details is to change from one medium to another. Most of
the time, the event has not been contrived by journalists, it has
'happened' but the public would have no knowledge of it if it
were not reported by the media. On the other hand, the media
have a limited share in the world of entertainment. People know
about theme parks, or sports grounds, or theatres because they

visit them or because they learn about them through the media; both approaches are complementary; the media induce their clients to make a visit; visitors revive their pleasure by seeing that place on the media. The music market is indiscriminate about what is broadcast and what is heard elsewhere, in discos, concert halls, supermarkets and pubs or on the beach. Unlike information, entertainment can be advertised; conversely, advertisement becomes, at times entertainment. This implies that customers are more active when selecting entertainment than when getting information. The world of information is self-centred; what it disseminates results from a compromise between politicians, news agencies, media moguls, reporters and journalists. The world of entertainment is open to its actual or potential consumers; it is intelligible only in the context of supply and demand. If we were content with analysing the messages conveyed by the media, the difference between information and entertainment would seem radical, which could induce us to ignore the latter. But if we consider people's attitudes we see that the recreational part of the media triggers more active reactions than their informatory part which makes it necessary to examine the media within the general framework of enjoyment such as it develops in contemporary societies.

CONFLICT AND NEGOTIATION

For many people, the mass media fulfill a precise function: they are designed to *convince* those who use them (to believe, to buy, to conform, etc.) and, in this respect, they are ideological tools paid and manipulated by the ruling class in order to reproduce and perpetuate the system which produced them. Ideology is another cumbersome word which has come to be loaded with negative connotations. We had better avoid it but it is so commonly used at the present time that we cannot get rid of it. Let us admit that, in this context, we shall call ideology the ways in which we view and make sense of ourselves and the world which surrounds us and also our relationship to other people or groups. Ideology includes all those activities that are concerned with the production of meaning or which contribute to influencing our thoughts or feelings. It implies signifying practices such as the regular purchase of a newspaper (even if we do not read it) or the daily switching on of our television set (even if we never watch it).

Propaganda and ideology

Ideology must be carefully differentiated from propaganda. The latter aims consciously at convincing (or cheating); it is a tool used by somebody for or against some well-defined result. The media, which participate in organized activities in support of different causes – political, humanitarian, commercial or whatever – do not stop disseminating propaganda and because people are permanently exposed to their messages, their real influence has often been overrated. A series of inquiries, initiated around the American sociologist Lazarsfeld,[16] then extended to other countries, has shown that few citizens change their voting intentions despite the election campaign. The old apprehension that opinion might be easily manipulated by propaganda has been succeeded by the 'minimal effects model' based on the discovery that the public is not very receptive to what it is told. Propaganda is no more than a variety of advertising and, as such, it can be easily denounced and criticized.

The distance between propaganda and ideology is well illustrated in a few lines written by a senior civil servant in 1937: 'We may take pride in observing that there is not a single film showing in London today which deals with any of the burning questions of the day.' What made the man proud was that, at least from his vantage point of view, the British government was not using the cinema to propagate its policy. But the fact that there were burning questions and that they should not be dealt with while people were enjoying themselves was another matter. Who determines what the urgent problems are? Nobody. What is urgent is what is felt urgent by a great many people who do not know each other but would agree spontaneously that this or that is top priority. And why is it good to divert people from urgent issues while they are in cinemas? To offer them a temporary escape from the real, the dirty and problematic everyday life? Deciding that the main purpose of entertainment is to introduce ordinary citizens into a different, nicer world is precisely an ideological choice.

This is a very crucial point in our analysis. It was already implied in Marx's critique of the ideological community, that is to say the community of values and norms which, in practice, brings together otherwise opposed classes such as the bourgeoisie and the proletariat. When the proletariat buy newspapers written by the bourgeoisie, they participate, unwittingly, in the ideological system of capitalism. The Marxist philosopher Louis Althusser has broadened and systematized Marx's theories.[17] According to Althusser, the sphere of ideology consists not only of the most obvious forms of intellectual practice, such as labelling other people, or defining what is 'right' and 'wrong'. It must be extended to the entire range of procedures and rites through which we experience our relationship with the others and make sense of our social existence, even in its purely material form. Take a habit as simple as switching on the television. A custom common to a great many viewers operates so as to produce within individuals who do exactly what their neighbours do a purely imaginative, therefore misleading conception of their place within the society. Althusser argues that such practices cannot be understood outside the social/economic context in which they are carried out. It is not what we read, but the very fact that we read this or that which demonstrates the efficacy of ideology.

Marxism aims at giving an exegis of objects in terms of previously identified opposite or conflicting interests and it provides us with clues which make it possible to 'read' the reality of social relationships in most of the artefacts fabricated by a society. Gangster (or detective) stories which we have already mentioned will help us understand how Marxists conceive of the relationship between the economic context and the media programmes. Detectives such as Dick Tracy and his like made their first appearance in the cartoon section of Sunday newspapers at the beginning of the 1930s. Attached to the police force of big cities threatened by a powerful gang they testified to the capacity of democratic societies to resist evil even provided they had recourse to unorthodox means. Their stories, often adapted from actual cases, proved so highly popular that radio and cinema picked them up. In an attempt to differ from the press, the gangster films of the 1930s and 1940s treated contemporary social issues with a touch of sympathy for the bad guys. Two points have to be stressed. On the one hand there is no doubt that written or filmed fiction reflected social concerns – drinking, delinquency, prostitution – but issues were simplified. Obvious connections, between gangsterism and politics or between the liquor trade and local power, for instance, were never mentioned. Provocative though it was, the exposition of economic problems was compensated for by traditional, reassuring solutions – good boys met pretty girls, the gangster was either killed or made amends. On the other hand, the depiction of the gangster (or detective) was an object of conflict between periodicals, radio and cinema, so that the features of the character varied according to the transactions carried out by the media in their search for an audience. The Marxists argue that the aftermath of the big crisis, which was experienced daily by many Americans, was a pretext to contrive an unstable, vague figure, the outcast, which could be reworked in many different ways. The gangster was an ideological fabrication. Why? Because the public, which identified in the stories in the newspapers or in films some reference to the contemporary situation, ascribed a personality to the fictional gangster who was merely an image and felt relieved because this malignant being was eliminated.

The power of ideology rests on the fact that people consider as natural what is, in fact, social. As we have said, information, such as is reported by the media, is the result of a bargain struck between the authoritative sources and the journalists. But the consumers do not realize that the newscast could be entirely different; they do not question the accuracy of what has been selected and is reproduced by all media. A very interesting point is that people are sometimes highly critical about the manner in which an event is being related, but do not question the fact that this very news item has been singled out. During the 1984/85 miners strike in Britain many people thought that the coverage of the situation was inadequate, biased, unfair, that too much emphasis was put on the management point of view but few of them ceased reading or listening to media.

The Marxist analysis of ideology is essential in many respects. It reminds us that most of us are excluded from the definition of what must be reported. A small group of experts decides for the vast majority, what is selected, sometimes for unscrupulous, opportunist reasons, which becomes what has to be told. We are therefore obliged to acknowledge the arbitrariness of information. What we read or hear is not necessarily what really matters. To a large extent, information begets information. Once a fact has been reported by a medium, the other media try to get new details, or new evidence. For some time, this event, which may have been unimportant, mobilizes public attention. The Falklands War and the Gulf War offer paradigmatic examples of a process of artificial expansion. Once they had decided to focus on military events, the media could not stop talking about war; the public was deluged with pictures and sounds more or less related to the conflict, the same facts were endlessly repeated, they were printed up to three times in the same issue of a newspaper, they were repeated again and again, every hour, on radio and television. What was purely ideological was not that the government defended its policy, which was no more than ordinary propaganda, but that everybody was obliged to hear about the war and was led to believe it was a vital issue.

Another puzzling thing is the interest the media arouse in people's minds. During the aforementioned wars, audiences, although they got no more than a tedious repetition of the same details, were hooked to their radios. The strength of ideology is reinforced by the fact that people swallow easily what they are told: it is not by chance that those addicted to television are called 'couch potatoes'.[18] Our understanding of our environment, the Marxists argue, depends not only upon our experience but upon how such experience is placed in a wider context – our town, our county, our nation, etc. The media offer representations or explanations which allow us to connect otherwise seemingly unrelated facts. For instance, by pouring out news about the war, they may incite us to believe that food shortage, transport delays and increases in prices are attributable to the conflict. The point, here, is that, in the battle for control of war news, the media do not try to deceive their customers. They do their job, which is to sell more than their competitors. But, in doing so, they mislead their public. We can go much further than that. Absence or silence are also ideological. The mass media rarely tell stories which might communicate the misery of the daily life in the poorest areas of the world. When a catastrophe does not urge them to indulge in sensationalism to reach a larger audience, they go to the other extreme of giving charming pictures of wild life in India or Africa. This is ideology: a discourse through which particular experiences are redefined and introduced in an apparently coherent whole.

Some analysts rightly object that Marxism does not account for many aspects of the consumption of media. When we look at a practice such as the regular viewing of television programmes we can, effectively, attempt to understand how its recurrence can 'mould' the viewers' mind to such an extent that they cannot bear any interruption and are satisfied with watching whatever they are being offered. But what allows us to state that consumers passively swallow the ideological message? What prevents us from assuming that readers/viewers are also likely to subvert ideology by deliberate selection and reinterpretation. It is true that science fiction programmes, that have been blossoming since the middle of the 1970s present a depressing vision of the future world, cramped with hooligans, drug pedlars, addicts or drunks, dominated by corrupt politicians and drug manufacturers and that they magnify the Batman-like heroes who will clean up the streets. But, depending on the personality of the readers/viewers, the reappearance of the same hoodlums in the same situation will trigger fear or laughter. Media consumption is a multifarious activity which cannot be reduced to one of its aspects and resists univocal interpretation.

Another shortcoming of the Marxist line of argument is that it tends to link all the media in an indiscriminate way, blurring the fact that rivalry may lead to significant divergence over the definition and presentation of events. During wars, unless censorship is very strict, contradictory statements are made by different media, provoking polemics which show that the media's opinions are at variance. Unless they are blind, media customers cannot ignore these debates.

I have mentioned the main counter-arguments opposed to Marxism but I think that they miss the point of the theory. This interpretation is based upon the presupposition that something deeper, more stable, what Marx called the mode of production, exists beyond ideology, in the social system by which and for the perpetuation of which it has been produced. When making fun of Rambo or of the contradictions between media, we are still immersed in the realm of ideology, we are attending to something which does not concern us, which has been devised by media manufacturers and prevents us from caring about our own business. Therefore, I find it useless to discuss Marxism. It is a powerful, developed system which may help us better to analyse the part the mass media play in perpetuating the system of power but had little to contribute towards an interpretation of the social function of the media.

The imaginary building of community

Marxism places the focus on large-scale processes, especially on the reproduction of social systems. When discussing it, very superficially, we mostly emphasized the fact that individual responses do no fit in with the system. Batman's admirers or mockers may be equally misled because they take notice of a phantasy but we cannot neglect the fact that they make use of this character in contrasting ways. For what purpose? We have already stressed

Weber's idea that people's behaviour must be understood according to the rationality which underlies and on which it is based.
Hence, the development of another model of interpretation which
does not ignore the validity of an external explanation but is
intent on analysing how human beings understand their practices.
Kaiser Wilhelm II desperately needed the approval of his subjects.
Constantly reading press clippings from all parts of Germany and
looking for news stories about himself, he found it painful when
they criticized him. Those journalists who were aware of this
were prone to reassure him. Both the newspapers and the sover-
eign were manipulating each other, thus creating a perfect circle
of deception. The adulation of the Kaiser masked urgent issues
such as the military policy of the Reich; it was an ideological
expedient. It was also rational to develop a discourse that most
Germans would agree with. In a country which had been unified
for a few years and was divided by political, geographical and
social oppositions, the Kaiser was a unifying force and the press
played a decisive part in offering topics for everyday conversation.

Let us be more specific about the presuppositions on which
this second model is grounded. Before being interpreted, a news
item has to be accepted by a community in which it can claim to
have an influence on the world. But communities are, to a large
extent, imaginary. They derive their particularity from the dangers
that threaten them or that they contrive, from the stories (or
gossip) which they generate and circulate. Their unity is
occasional rather than firmly based and one which needs to be
continuously reaffirmed. Many uncertainties are inherent in such
an act of imagination. It is therefore necessary to create statements or narratives likely to reinforce the sense of 'commonness'
and enable every member to manifest their belonging to the
group. Such communities where people have to confirm and
reinforce their values offer an intersubjective guarantee of
acceptability as well as a limit to the tolerable interpretations
of the news. This may sound a bit too abstract. A concrete
example will show what is at stake here. Why is it that the
collapse of the Soviet system and the consequent events that took
place at such dramatic speed in 1990 were not foreseen? After
reunification, there was a bitter indictment of the western media
in Germany where they were accused of having developed a
passive, dilatory attitude to the question of national unity.
Journalists were castigated for concealing the failure of the East

German republic and convincing everybody in the west that the division of Europe into two 'blocs' was virtually impossible to bring down. Many documents support that view,[19] but they also show that if the media actually supported the policy of the federal government which believed that a divided Germany was the foundation of the Cold War status quo, the government in turn was fooled by the media which argued against reunification as a fatal regression to the past. In other words, government policy was underpinned by opinions developed in the media and vice versa. The general drift away from the idea of unity was, undoubtedly, an ideological choice but it was manipulated neither by the media nor by those in power. It arose from a common anxiety regarding the future of the Federal Republic.

Truth is not in question, here, nor the meaning of the stories which are told. The act of interpretation will constitute, more or less in agreement, the same reading of the events, although the sameness cannot be attributed to the very content of the text but to the collective nature of the interpretative act. Any medium makes sense for one or several communities whose explanatory work (i.e. work done to interpret the news) is at the same time assimilative because it integrates what is told in the texts, and self-transforming because the texts modify the vision of the world previously accepted by the members of the group. The media create or arrange objects or facts so as to imply meanings and emotions according to the conventions shared by a given society and these objects/facts elicit meaningful inferences in those who possess at least minimal competence in the same cultural universe. In any group where media circulate, people are more sensitive to the context of their own media consumption than to the logic or content of the texts.

However, the media do not obliterate all the differences, Georg Simmel has strongly emphasized the importance of competition and differentiation in the evolution of social groups.[20] Communities are characterized, in Simmel's view, by a permanent struggle between groups or factions for the categories and distinctions on which understanding is based. In this respect we must question the widely accepted idea that the main meaningful difference between the media are the technology which produces them (printed/broadcast, words/pictures, etc.) and their content. We would rather say that they have to be differentiated according to the communities which can accept and understand them. In other words, we must try to understand where the media gather

their information from, how to display it and what are the social
settings and situations typically associated with their use.

Conflicting though they are, the two models – the Marxist
one and the model adapted from Weber and Simmel – are not
exclusive. It must only be stressed that they do not aim at the
same thing. The former, based on a system of critical concepts
provides an insight into social relationships taken in their broad-
est sense. The latter aims at getting an inner understanding of
feelings and concerns that the members of a group have in
common. Deciding between them is a matter of strategy: the
former allows the media to be defined in the logic of capitalism,
the latter tries to capture the interweaving of media propositions
and creative individual reactions.

Media provide us with snapshots of the world, but is there
any consistency in these images? A critical point of view of the
press, developed since the end of the eighteenth century and later
extended to radio and television, has influenced the research on
the function of the methods of disseminating information. Media
culture, it is assumed, has become elevated into a powerful source
of imagery and illusion. It is easier to make political points in
game-show formats than in serious debates and many programmes select their personalities from showbusiness; the politicians must speak even if they have nothing to say (it is part of
their job) – it is the television mongers who make them take part
in their programmes. What is offered by the media could best be
symbolized by the classic pantomime witch who disappears in a
puff of smoke, laughing, having left the Miller's daughter to turn
gold into straw rather than the other way round: all we get are
illusions that are enjoyable, even fascinating, as we watch the
story unfold but which, afterwards, make us feel guilty for having
spent so much time absorbing so much trivia.

The critical view of the media proceeds from a close analysis
of a few productions. It is true that many press articles and many
radio and television discussions are rather banal and do not tell
us very much. But all these items are elements of a whole and a
thorough examination of the details fails to capture the medium
as such. From the eighteenth century until the present day, mankind has been witnessing simultaneously the progressive transformation of the environment and the expansion of the methods
of disseminating information. The change has been discontinuous
and uneven, faster and earlier in some areas than in others, but
it has increased the range of opportunities available to societies,

creating an unprecedented situation. Mass media are neither good nor bad, they are facilities and, like any facility, can be misused. Sociologists are not entrusted with evaluating media shortcomings; they must study them in the socio-cultural whole of which they are part. In the first chapter, we saw that the current use of a medium creates a 'mechanical' relationship between the consumers. This statement now has to be completed. The content of the media provides people with insight into their own environment and also into other, much wider issues and it brings them entertainment. What is conveyed by a medium thus becomes a frame of reference. This does not imply that the audience's knowledge of the world is determined by messages diffused by the media. Starting from the same reports of the same events people can reach different conclusions between which no compromise is possible. Hence the question which is addressed in this chapter: how do people integrate what the media tell them into their own experience?

NOTES

1 An expression coined by B. Mazlish, *A New Science: the Breakdown of Connections and the Birth of Sociology*, (1990, Oxford University Press) who shows that the pessimistic vision developed in the middle of the nineteenth century has influenced most ensuing attempts to understand the aftermath of industrial changes. In Mazlish's view, sociology, when it was born, tried to tackle the same problem from a more systematic, less subjective and pessimistic point of view.

2 And also a large portion of what we learn about the world. It is accepted that one hour after the announcement of President Kennedy's shooting, the majority of Americans had been informed, mostly by telephone calls from relatives or friends. The trouble is that checking is difficult in this field.

3 E. Durkheim, *The Division of Labour in Society* (1893, Eng. trans. 1964, London, Collier-Macmillan).

4 E. Bowen, *The House in Paris* (1935, London, Penguin, p. 39).

5 A point of view developed by B. A. Dobkin, *Tales of Terror. Television News and the Construction of the Terrorist Threat* (1992, New York, Praeger), who thinks that the State Department induced the television networks to present terrorism as part of a war against America.

6 See J. F. MacDonald, *Television and the Red Menace: The*

Video Road to Vietnam (1985, New York, Prager); D. Hallin, *The Uncensored War: The Media and Vietnam* (1989, Berkeley, University of California Press); M. Anderegg (ed.), *Inventing Vietnam: The War in Film and Television* (1991, Philadelphia, Temple University Press); B. Cumings, *War and Television* (1992, New York, Verso).

7 On this very complex issue, see P. Schlesinger, *Putting 'Reality' Together: BBC News* (1979, London, Constable) and H. Gans, *Deciding what's News: A Study of CBS Evening News, NBC Nightly News, Newsweek and Time* (1980, New York, Vintage Books).

8 R. Donovan and R. Scherer, *Unsilent Revolution: Television News and American Public Life, 1948–1991* (1992, Cambridge University Press).

9 D. Dayan and E. Katz, *Media Events. The Live Broadcasting of History* (1992, Cambridge, London, Harvard University Press, p. 179).

10 C. Geraghty, *Women and Soap Opera: A Study of Prime Time Soaps* (1991, Oxford, Polity Press).

11 Soap production which used extensively simple elements such as soda and chlorine, was one of the first heavy industries; it made colossal profits which were partially invested in advertisement. Hence the label of 'soaps' bestowed on serials sponsored by industrial companies.

12 M. Schudson, in *Advertising: The Uneasy Persuasion. Its Dubious Impact on American Society* (1993, London, Routledge) explains lucidly how advertising works or fails to work according to the public's response.

13 S. Kaminsky and J. H. Mahan, *American Television Genres* (1985, Chicago, Nelson Hall Inc.) p. 22 ff.

14 A nickname conceived by R. Sklar, *City Boys, Cagney, Bogart, Garfield* (1992, Princeton, University Press).

15 Transistors = transductance resisters, substances such as germanium which control the flow of the electric current. The first radio transistors appeared in the United States in 1954.

16 P. F. Lazarsfeld, B. Berelson and H. Gaudet, *The People's Choice* (1968, London, New York, Columbia University Press).

17 L. Althusser, 'Ideology and ideological state apparatuses' (in *Lenin and Philosophy and other Essays* 1971, London, New Left Books).

18 A very interesting expression whose origins are telling. The

American 'tube' soon became 'boob tube', 'tube' suggested 'tuber'; it could then have been turnip or carrot but potato matched very well with crisp, crunch and eventually couch.

19 A good sample of media documents is critically analysed in J. Hacker's *Deutsche Irrtümer Schönfarber und Helfershelfer der SED-Diktatur in Westen* (1992, Berlin, Ulstein).

20 'Differentiation and the principle of energy saving', in P. Lawrence, *Georg Simmel: Sociologist and European* (1976, Sunbury, Nelson) pp. 129–32.

3
Media makers

From a financial point of view, media production does not seem to have a very important position in contemporary economies. 'Does not seem' – because it is extremely difficult to provide accurate statistics and make clear-cut statements about these matters. Most companies are intent on keeping their income a secret. Even public service broadcasting has its secrets, official budgets are available but money is seldom spent as originally planned. Free markets or the establishment are not totally responsible for this lack of information. The production of media items is characterized by extreme flexibility and a rather unusual division of labour. Some firms integrate writing, printing and distribution. Others have recourse to specialized companies which act as intermediaries between advertisers and the media, or between the producers and their clientele. There are also all-purpose companies that undertake accountancy or management consultancy, and also publish magazines. Who will ever disentangle the various sources of profit of such companies? Estimating the number of people working regularly in the media is almost impossible. It is well known that employing regular staff costs more money than employing people on a short-term basis and this is especially true in the media, where it is necessary to adapt quickly to the variations in audience sizes. Media companies live both in a state of constant expansion and under a permanent threat of crisis which forces them to commissioning work, most of which is carried out by independent producers who, in turn, work alternately for the media or, for example, advertising. The dissemination of information is an evolutionary process. It would be much easier to deal with a static world of news made by independent, competing media. But that kind of equilibrium has never existed; change has always been the central issue. Despite the lack of accurate statistics we may assume that the media contribute less than 5 per cent of the Gross National Product in countries where they have been present for a long period and in some cases their contribution falls under 2 per cent. It is hardly surprising that the media fall far behind the industrial sector but they also fall behind service industries such as banking or communications.

Media entrepreneurs complain that they are always losing money, some of them hinting that their deficit amounts to more than one thousand million pounds a year. Yet, they fight hard to increase their power and create a monopoly, thus eliminating weaker entrepreneurs and contributing to the blurring of the panorama of news production. The media have become the site of a permanent war between various social or political interests. Any government will be keen to keep an eye on the media but many other forces – banks, industry, trade unions, lobbies of various sorts and more obscure organizations would also like to have their share in the dissemination of information. What is the nature of this strange world where money seems less important than power and influence? What is the role of different firms and different lobbies in the diffusion of news? These are the questions we should try to tackle now.

STRATEGIES

It is generally accepted that the shaping of news stories is crucial in shaping public attitude to current problems and it is assumed that the media are a considerable influence on opinion, especially when people have no access to alternative sources of information. All participants in the debates about the power of media display an affected naïvety in defending the rights of the public. Since they agree that the impact of information is considerable, the question most media producers face is how best to use it for everyone's sake. The media thus crystallize commonplace ideas concerning people's reactions. Commentators do not point out how difficult it is to determine a link between media content and audience behaviour. Most of them prefer to theorize about how mass media help 'construct' audiences, especially the popular classes, as obedient citizens and active participants in a consumer society. However, what little evidence there is does not suggest that the media make, or do not make an especially significant impact on public opinion. The key process in this field is that of self-legitimation whereby producers of information strive to persuade their potential audience that they care mostly about its needs and also that they speak the language of rationality and truth. If we are to understand the aims of the media mongers, we must forget for the time being what they reveal about themselves. Starting from an analysis of the competition between those who provide news we shall now try to investigate the strategies these people construct.

Controlling the media

Who ought to run the media? A fundamental difference confronts those who defend the concept of public information and those who champion a free market. Of course, both invoke ideas of fairness to explain their policy. The former contend that professionalism and neutrality are the most essential qualities while the latter stress the importance of unconventionality, free choice and liberty. Those who defend the theories of independence (= public) or liberty (= private) search for a guiding principle to regulate the distribution of information in a society. In reality, their rhetoric is remote, not only from their actual practice but also from the ideas that guide their management of information. An issue often tackled in these debates is quality. Can commercial producers who commission freelance employees to make their programmes achieve the same standards as those of highly trained public broadcasting full-time staff? Conversely, can public broadcasting be as sharp and incisive as that of the free market? To take a particular example, no-one has ever denied the rigorousness of BBC documentaries. But, if they are loaded down with social concerns, they often lack the wide appeal of independent documentaries, which may be less perfect but seem dramatic, are gripping and address urgent problems. Contenders develop a rhetoric in which everyone is the guardian of public interest. They thus avoid the fundamental question of the bias both systems introduce into their programmes, despite their respective claims – a state-controlled medium is not necessarily honest; a private one is not always independent. Let us be more specific. London Radio Service, a British government news management station, broadcasts official documents such as new regulations, ministerial speeches and parliamentary reports. It also produces its own news bulletins which it provides free to any other medium. Newspapers, radio or television stations use the material as if it were their own, thus disseminating as independent information what is, in fact, a government version of events. Purely commercial media boast to being much freer than official broadcasting but they are strictly dependent upon their sponsors. Advertisers do not like programmes which attract large audiences consisting predominantly of people, such as children or elderly people, who will not buy expensive goods. Market-led media often decide to restrict access to entertainment; for instance, in many cases, cable television, which reaches a limited but affluent portion of the population, buy the exclusive rights to popular events (e.g. sporting events), which would be likely to attract large audiences. As can be inferred from the example of the London Radio Service, there is no radical divergence of principle and procedure between the public and private sectors. Opposed though they are or pretend to be, they cannot ignore each other. There is permanent interplay between the media industries, the government and the consumers. Interference is partly specific to the functioning of information making, since the same news is, necessarily, reported by almost all media at the same time. It is also more general because it has to do with the evolution of the world market where information is permanently sold or exchanged.

One of the aims of our research is to look in some detail at how the confrontation between various information makers works in different places, to try to explain what has led to one of the possible answers (for instance, public service, or private ownership) being chosen rather than another and to assess the consequences of using the different systems. We must begin by stating that the traditional dichotomy, public/private, is artificial, and is not sufficient to classify the producers of news. After a compromise was reached between public and private television broadcasting in the United Kingdom (1954)[1] some companies which were not part of the deal began attacking what they called the 'duopoly'. This was simply a way of trying to compete with the

two existing networks, the BBC and ITV. Given the permeability
of national frontiers and the fact that it is difficult to prevent the
reception of foreign broadcasting in democratic countries, no real
monopoly can be established in the dissemination of information.
The realm of media is one of permanent bargaining where information gatherers, public as well as private, have to find some
mutually acceptable solution that allows them to pursue their
interests in the best possible way. It is true that, for various
reasons (huge investments, expansion of some leading companies)
which will be examined later, there has always been a tendency
towards a centralization of the national media. But, simultaneously, modern technology has helped launch crudely printed
magazines, masses of pamphlets and leaflets and crudely drawn
comics and 'free' radio and television stations. Instead of merely
two, three sectors can be distinguished in the management of
mass media: the governmental, the commercial and the
communal.

An important aspect of the relationship between a society
and its media is that once a compromise has been found between
conflicting interests, media producers and governments alike seek
to maintain it and attempt to demonstrate that it is the best
solution. As ordinary citizens do not know how mass media
function in other countries, they tend to believe that theirs is the
'normal' system. This continues until another agreement has to be
reached. Then, the new organization becomes the norm; everyone
thinks it has its equivalent in other countries. In reality, some of
the country-by-country contrasts are impressive. They enable us
to move away from the abstract debates about independence or
objectivity. As radio broadcasting expanded very quickly, in less
than a decade, at the outset of the 1920s, its history provides us
with an ideal example to identify the interest groups involved in
the selling of information and to understand how the three above-
mentioned sectors could develop simultaneously in different surroundings.

Radio, and later television, in Britain was soon given the
social and institutional form of a quasi-state organization. This
was not, initially, the result of a political choice. The manufacturers of the receiving equipment who were eager to sell the
material they had produced during the war formed a broadcasting
company (1922) and came to an arrangement with the Post Office
which had the monopoly of wireless transmission. Radio was
already operating when discussions of control and operation of

radio in the public interest began. Many politicians or opinion leaders who were frightened by the rapid expansion of revolutionary ideas[2] presented the state as the only possible safeguard against abuses of democracy. Others stressed the social duties of the state, which had to educate the citizens, offer them healthy entertainment and elevate public taste. These debates resulted in the creation, in 1926, of the British Broadcasting Corporation. The initial company, which had the monopoly of broadcasting but which was only trying to create a demand for equipment and did not care about the programme content, was replaced by a centralized national system which was not much interested in local needs and expectations but was prone to guide public opinion firmly.[3] As a radio historian has noted, the BBC's blistering eagerness to take responsibility was confused with an innate capacity to exercise it.[4]

In the United States, as in most countries, the first networks were set up by big companies which merely intended to make a profit. General Electric and the Columbia Phonograph Company, which had surplus goods to sell and American Telegraphs and Telephones, which wanted to rent out its long cables launched the first American networks – the National Broadcasting Company (NBC) and the Columbia Broadcasting System (CBS). Later the antitrust laws forced NBC to sell one of its subsidiaries which became the American Broadcasting Company (ABC). A few government bodies, the Navy and the Post Office, advocated a state monopoly but the federal administration was not intent on controlling information so that private companies could easily out pace its shaky attempts at regulation. The Radio Act that the Congress passed in 1927 was content with granting freedom of speech and banning censorship.[5] By the late 1920s the network-dominated, advertising-supported system was firmly established in the USA. A public broadcasting service was launched to explore topics that did not interest commercial radio. Its quality and seriousness were acknowledged but it didn't threaten (and never intended to threaten) the pre-eminence of the profit-making sector.

The solution adopted in the Netherlands not only instances the development of a system different to those which prevailed in Britain or in the United States but also provides a paradigmatic example of an arrangement which is widespread where small communities (towns, unions, local societies) are concerned. Broadcasting began very early on in the Netherlands and organizations affiliated to the three main political forces – Catholics, Protestants and Socialists – were keen on using the new medium. The most technically minded of their members thought that it would be possible to build broadcasting stations of their own but this turned out to be much too expensive. A national broadcasting service was created which was entrusted with transmitting the output of independent radio stations commissioned by the political parties. Consumer groups composed of members belonging to the three main forces managed their respective networks, which were financed by licence fees paid by the listeners. This arrangement guaranteed a good transmission system and prevented disputes between users of a particular frequency.

High principles do not account for the rapid adoption of these three notably different systems. Instead, we have to consider the more important issues of economic resources, technical achievements, political bargaining, supply of and demand for information or entertainment. Money was the most important factor. Although money is a crucial aspect of broadcasting, other factors such as political or editorial issues have temporarily eclipsed its importance in the history of radio. Nevertheless, money was the very origin of broadcasting. However, it is no surprise that regular broadcasting began very early in Britain, the United States and the Netherlands, where electrical industries were powerful. Conversely radio developed much later in regions such as Australia where it would have helped to reach scattered centres of population but where there was no industrial incentive to create it. The influence of the big companies was not limited to the launching of radio networks. Radio could have evolved in a rather different way, for instance, as a medium for collective listening in public theatres, as was experimented with in Fascist Italy[6] but the consequent drop in the production of radio sets would not have met manufacturers' expectations. Political issues also played a decisive part in the deal. In 1920, long-distance transmission was already secured by telephone and the conditions upon which wireless could be used were precisely defined. Regulation, such as it existed before broadcasting began, influenced radio's early development in accordance with pre-existing laws which had not been passed for radio. In some countries, the state assumed responsibility for transmission, while in others, it was left up to private companies. Finance was a third determining factor. It was impossible to launch a new medium, especially an expensive one such as radio, without appropriate investment in equipment, programmes and transmission. Since no network could rely totally upon public funding, money had to come from advertising, from individual subscriptions given by affiliated members or from a licence fee. Here, again, there were problems. With a state monopoly the tax for this service was paid to the government, which might be tempted to retain a percentage. Generosity and donations from interested parties subordinated the networks to individuals or companies, for example, of a particular political persuasion, who thus had enough power to influence a network and even change its line. Depending on advertising was also risky and was likely to trigger off a conflict with the press. All these difficulties were swiftly overcome thanks to harsh bargaining between a limited number of experts. The claims of public interest were constantly evoked but nobody ever bothered to interview a panel of would-be listeners. People were extremely interested in the potential of the new medium but since they gave little thought to its financial management, they were not given the information. On the whole, audiences approved of the status given to radio in their respective countries.

Mass media and social domination

We cannot be content with simply listing dates and events, they have to be seen through a sociological viewfinder which pinpoints the interrelatedness of the agents (governments, big companies, communities) involved in the deals, and their relationship to audiences. The coming of radio resembles, on a reduced scale, what had previously happened to the press and what has been the dominant trend in the evolution of mass media since the eighteenth century, namely the tendency towards monopoly by a few people. Two overlapping and distinctive logics are involved in the process – the logic of profit and the logic of indefinite expansion. The two phenomena interweave and obscure each other's outline but they are, at least partially independent and, for a start, profits have to be carefully separated from monopoly. At the end of the nineteenth century, a handful of entrepreneurs successfully utilized technical innovations to produce cheap newspapers for a mass readership. Simultaneously they tried to gather as many newspapers as possible in one firm. Correlation must not be mistaken for causality; the former operation did not imply the latter. When a profitable means of information is bought by another company, it could keep going but, most of the time, management as well as guiding principles and information sources are transferred to the buyer which may result in a loss in audience, for customers no longer find what they were used to getting every day. What is then the significance of monopoly?

In most business the aims have always been to gain as much money as possible but such is not necessarily the case where media are concerned. Lord Beaverbrook, the proprietor of the *Daily Express* and one of the most influential tycoons of the interwar period, confessed very frankly that his purpose in running a paper was not to increase his profits but to disseminate his ideas. The main goal in the realm of media is to dominate the world of information. Who will purchase the next available newspaper or television network? The winner will have widened their control while the loser will be confined to a lesser audience. The struggle for the control of media reflects ambitions which go much beyond purely economic profits – media mongers want to increase their influence, preserve their position against potential rivals and win a position of domination.

The concept of rationality which, behind Weber, we consider to be central to sociology prevents us from thinking this is erratic behaviour. It must be stressed, here, that information is always connected with power. Brute power in the case of dictatorships where 'news' is propaganda. Here, the official line on any problem is handed down daily from the highest levels and reporters who do not follow the line risk losing their job. Freedom of speech which is non-existent and even inconceivable in authoritarian systems is not a universal characteristic of human societies but rather a characteristic of commercial societies where the permanent flow of exchanges includes the commerce of information. Overt control and coercion are therefore less obvious in liberal countries than in dictatorships and they may even be abolished because they are both ineffective and useless. During the first half of the nineteenth century the English government, fearing popular insurrection, imposed a series of taxes which should have killed off the radical newspapers. These papers survived because they were cheaply manufactured and because there was a public for them. But, later, they disappeared because they could not sustain the cost of industrialization. The liberalization of information has never resulted from the benevolence of the rulers; it has always reflected both shifts in what is considered to be dangerous for the powerful and conflicts or compromise between those who disseminate information.

The struggle to control the press and broadcasting in liberal systems cannot be understood without reference to the nature of supply in the media market. Information concentrates largely on what is commonly taken to be politics, that is to say the activity of choosing the government and then filling the offices of state. This is only a limited part of a country's activities which does not interfere much with people's ordinary lives. But this is what politicians are concerned with. However, journalists consider it their specific job to provide their public with details about the political system and to comment on them. Politicians and journalists necessarily talk to each other and develop mutual, if often conflictual relations. Already in the nineteenth century newspaper publishers unanimously regarded the power of defining news as the foundation of their social influence and a prize to be jealously guarded. A close link between political parties and the press was characteristic of the Victorian era; both governments and oppositions could then rely with certainty on their respective organs and use them to advertise their programmes. The technical and editorial upheaval which took place during that period has generally been called 'the Northcliffe revolution'. However, Northcliffe was only one among the media moguls who modernized the press, but he became a symbol because of his deep involvement in politics. Northcliffe was a perfect example of the authority conferred upon a politician by his commitment to information. The development of audiovisual media in the twentieth century has slackened the party allegiance of the newspapers without modifying their permanent relationship to the political leaders. The boards of media companies include representatives of political parties as well as former top civil servants. Apart from the prestige that they bring to the corporation, these men are often in a position to give precious advice and make delicate negotiations work easier.

Despite their permanent connection with politicians the media mongers do not need to interfere in affairs of state; they may enjoy a deep influence without exercising a direct power. This is best understood if we bear in mind the distinction established by Max Weber between power and domination. Power, Weber argues, is linked to authority. It implies the possibility of imposing a rule upon other people and the duty, for these people, to obey. It was because they hold the power that, in the same period, governments opted for free broadcasting in some countries and for a state monopoly in other countries. There were then many possible solutions. The state made a choice and whatever the decision was, public opinion agreed. Domination is merely an influence deriving from a position and acting upon other people who are formally free to refuse but find it more convenient or more rewarding to accept. 'Domination may be based on the most diverse motives of compliance: all the way from simple habituation to the most rational calculation of advantage'[7] which implies that domination cannot exist without a minimum of voluntary compliance. The media moguls have no authority. Even when they are in a position of monopoly, no-one is forced to buy their products and their enterprise is doomed to failure unless customers, rationally seeking information or entertainment, pay their money. Weber is fully aware of the fact that profits are often a consequence of domination and contribute to reinforce it, but he is intent on making it clear that those who are in a dominant position do not apply it, usually, to the pursuit of purely economic ends. The possession of one or several media is mostly instrumental inasmuch as it may provide the owner with a wider influence. Media moguls are not primarily oriented towards profits; they want to extend their domination and it is enough for them that things evolve in the direction more profitable to their interest.

What differentiates the media from other products likely to ensure industrial tycoons a real influence is that they are closely linked to the realm of politics. As has already been noted, current affairs are the favourite topic of the press and broadcasting. Governments are interested in keeping in touch with the media and controlling information about their actions. One of their basic aims is to prevent the emergence of ideas subversive to authority and they meet with little resistance from those who own the media business, for these people generally share the same political leanings as the political leaders and, at any rate, are keen on preventing legal prosecution. Critical comments can even be welcome. They are better than silence, for they stress the importance of political debate. Politicians, who are at first reluctant to being interviewed or do not want to be involved in audience-participation programmes learn quickly to steer clear of danger. What matters is to be present. Regardless of what they say, politicians improve their reputation by appearing in a particular medium: if they are named, it means that they are important people and deserve attention.

Except in periods of crisis, governments pursue a non-interventionist line while retaining a degree of indirect control over the media. Public authorities are often blamed for restricting freedom of information but far from being a state instrument, censorship often participates in commercial strategies. The British Board of Film Censors was established in 1913, not by the government but by the production companies themselves. It was officially meant to suppress, or modify 'indecent' films and to control the spread of politically subversive ideas. The producers had come to the conclusion that a censorship of scripts would cost them less than cuts or an outright ban imposed after production. At the same time censorship would enable the biggest companies to control the industry at the expense of smaller, or avant-garde producers. Censorship did not aim primarily at limiting the freedom of cinema; it was a good economic device.[8] Similarly, in the United States, the Hays Office, a trade organization to censor films, was formed in 1922 by the major American producers to convince various religious, family, moral organizations that Hollywood films were perfectly safe and could be shown to everybody. In both cases, decisions aimed at consolidating the box office were taken without any interference of the government but in the closest cooperation with lobbies and churches.

The fear of state interference has long haunted the media mongers, especially during the moments of social or diplomatic unrest, and has prompted them to be very cautious. All through these periods, the media moguls have agreed to voluntary systems of censorship; they have also stayed in close contact with the political authorities and have offered to back them. In June 1938, that is before the Czech crisis led Europe to the brink of war, the Newsreels Association of Great Britain emphasized, in a memo, 'the readiness of all the newsreel companies to assist the government and public departments on all suitable occasions in reproducing items deemed to be of public interest'.[9] However, the extent of official intervention, at least in free societies, must not be overrated. Only a small number of posters, articles and films have ever advertised the official policy. Far from issuing solely war-related items, the media have not suppressed or even reduced the space dedicated to entertainment or general information during the two world wars. In short, governments seldom impose severe restrictions on the dissemination of news since the media themselves are intent on avoiding anything potentially dangerous to national security.

Governments' interest in media is not limited to the local market; it is even more oriented towards foreign than towards domestic propaganda. As soon as films started to be made, various national authorities encouraged and commissioned documentary films to capture what was meant to be the most significant, attractive features of any country. After the United States entered the First World War, the government appointed a propaganda agency, the Committee on Public Information which attempted to advertise abroad, not only the diplomatic aims of the White House but also of America itself, its scenic beauty, its dynamism, its industrial performance. During the Second World War the American Office of War Information imposed a code according to which movies should give a positive picture of America; a film like *Casablanca* was, for instance, officially commended for showing the United States as 'the haven of the oppressed and homeless'. Very soon these efforts went beyond victory and attempted to settle the American economy on the world market. Even in peaceful times, foreign offices of most countries keep an eye on the image of their nation circulating abroad. The media of other countries are their main, sometimes their unique source of information. Embassies, which cannot intervene directly, spend a great deal of money and energy in trying to influence the journalists or film producers. They also campaign to paint a favourable portrait of their country by distributing films or papers which illustrate the best tourist attractions or describe economic achievements.

Modern governments need media to advertise their policy domestically and abroad. Information is part of the structure of power relations, it helps circulate a positive image of statesmen and politicians. However, the media companies are not amorphous amplifiers of dominant ideas. They happen sometimes to clash with public authorities, for instance, when means of information owned or financed by the state challenge them too seriously or when the tax policy is accused of favouring one medium against the others. Governments and media moguls are therefore bound to bargain constantly. When NBC was founded, in 1926, its board proclaimed that it would work 'so that every event of national importance may be broadcast widely throughout the United States'. This sounds very fair; there is a patriotic theme in the statement. But it is the press or the broadcasting networks that decide what is 'of national importance' and will disseminate it. Consequently, the White House must reckon with the media. Of course, governments can make reprisals. For instance, antitrust laws allow the American authorities to limit the expansion of media companies. In the United Kingdom and in many countries, broadcasting organizations have to obtain rechartering periodically and are obliged to bargain with the state. Both sets of institutions – the legitimate power and the media – need each other, are linked in their common struggle for domination and are intent on maintaining reciprocal support. To boot, the various connections, personal as well as institutional, which exist between media owners and the ruling class make matters much easier. Exciting though they are, polemics between those who emphasize the necessary protection of media freedom from interference by the state and those who think that this freedom cannot survive without an interventionist state sound, therefore, a bit abstract. The state is invested with a legitimacy which enables it to enforce its authority. In this respect there is an imbalance between the political power and any other kind of social influence and it is only thanks to the consent of the state that the media have developed into a huge industry, increasingly large and expensive. But this does not involve reciprocal mistrust for the state and most corporate organizations are bound to cooperate.

Conflicts are often brutal in the world of information but they take place inside the realm of the media where contending groups do not stop struggling for domination. These battles which have developed since the birth of mass media, in past centuries, have been driven and shaped by the rise of industrial capitalism. During the various periods of technological evolution, different groups have alternately controlled a vast portion of the market and then lost their monopoly. We have begun with an analysis of external strategies, we must now proceed to see how the media companies manage their internal problems.

NETWORKS

One of the most intriguing paradoxes of the media is that those who produce them share the same ideas about the ranking in importance of the various events going on in the world. Many things 'happen' at any one time; masses of details and facts do not stop coming into editorial offices. Since deciding which facts to reject and which ones to select is a hazardous business, there should be extremely different information programmes. However, despite the lack of objectivity in the nature of what is told to the public, there seems to be a given list of ultimate news values on which everybody involved in the system will agree. The scheduling of the radio and television channels is uncannily similar with the same news broadcast simultaneously. How can we account for this paradox? A partial answer can be found in the previous section, where we have shown how politicians and media moguls converge on the definition of what matters. We must now look at media enterprises to see how they get their information and how they reshape it for their public.

News agencies

Where does a news item come from? How do newspapers, radio and television manage to announce the same event, at the same time, in different countries? They all depend on news agencies, which are their main source, and which, apart from purely local information, have a monopoly in deciding what is worthwhile internationally and even nationally.

News agencies are not only central to the control that they exert over the definition and dissemination of news, they also encapsulate the most significant features of the world of information. There are few of them, to begin with: Reuters in the United Kingdom, Associated Press and United Press International in the United States, Tass in Russia, Agence France-Presse in France. News agencies face the same problems as most of the media: it is hard for them to make their books balance on information alone. Collecting news and diffusing it as soon as possible is extremely expensive. In the second half of the nineteenth century a few New York newspapers, willing to crush lesser papers, formed a consortium – Associated Press (AP). AP negotiated a contract with the Western Union telegraph company which had a virtual monopoly of the United States' Cables. Costly though it was, the deal gave the consortium the power to control the distribution of news within a constantly increasing area. During four decades journalistic success was measured, in part, by one's ability to get hold of the AP news reports. At the beginning of the twentieth century Reuters made huge investments to monopolize the transatlantic cable. By allowing it to sell its exclusive news the direct service between two continents strengthened Reuters' worldwide influence. Throughout the present century news agencies have been challenged by advances in modern technology. Thanks to communication satellites any event can be announced everywhere while it is happening. If they want to keep competitive, the agencies have to be the most technically advanced in collecting and immediately rediffusing news so that the fastest way for a Berlin newspaper to be informed of what is on in the town is through an agency. This implies huge investment in equipment and in staff for, contrary to what is often thought, the computerization of information processing requires much manpower: to take but an example, Reuters' staff increased two-fold when modern management was introduced.

Those who get the news pay for it but the international agencies need more than this cash to survive. France-Presse and Tass are financially backed by their respective governments. Reuters was long subsidized by the Foreign Office and the BBC.[10] When it became perfectly obvious that there was no way to make the diffusion of general news pay, the British agency achieved its independence by diversifying its activities as the American companies had previously done. Reuters has become the leading purveyor of stock exchange quotations to the world financial markets, the profits of the financial services making up for the losses in the information sector.

Although getting information is expensive, agencies cannot give it up. The ability to define news has always been seen by governments and, more importantly, by stockmarkets as a source of international domination which has to be maintained at any cost. During both world wars the belligerents that had news agencies gained enormous advantage from their dominance of international information and in particular their ability to control the news which, via neutral countries, reached the opposition. The capacity to excise from their system any press or broadcasting group which appears to be antagonistic gives news agencies enormous power. Conversely, the advantage of affiliation to an international agency cannot be ignored by any medium.

This leads to a harsh competition between agencies, which is also typical of the world of media. AP was founded because the newspapers which belonged to the consortium could not only gain preferential telegraph rates but could also exclude their rivals from access to national and international stories: success was created as well as rewarded by such affiliation; customers became used to buying newspapers mostly for their AP membership. It was this strangulation of non-affiliated papers which finally overwhelmed the system. The monopoly of small groups of powerful metropolitan papers served by the AP decayed once a successful challenge could be mounted by United Press and by William Randolph Hearst's International News Service – both businesses with greater flexibility than their monolithic rival. Later, Hearst's agency lost its market, like many other services which were too small to survive. The monopoly shared by the 'big five' does not mean that there is no more competition. The main agencies do not stop trying to increase their clientele at the expense of the other. They are also threatened by new services such as CNN (Cable News Network), with its 24-hour broadcasting that provides up-to-date information in words and pictures. If they want to survive in a world where electronic communications reduce the value of instant news, the agencies are bound to diversify their activities. Harsh competition implies recourse to modern technology. This implies a permanent hunt for investors and shareholders, concentration becoming thus the most salient characteristics of news agencies. It is true that they still play a crucial role in defining and disseminating information, but it must not be forgotten that informing is no longer either their main task or their main source of finance.

Corporations

The basic communication scheme as it is generally described in media studies, involves three elements: the emitter who decides what information is worthwhile, the medium which gives the message its form and the addressee. The model is probably too simplistic but it is not at variance with the ideas about audiences and about the messages conveyed by the media that have already been discussed. However, media organizations and news agencies that have just been described do not fit in with the pattern for it is impossible to integrate them in any of the three above-mentioned elements. Marx, who was himself a journalist and an expert in media business was the first to emphasize the tendency to separate financial management from editorship. He explained that the rise of industrial capitalism was leading to the incorporation of the means of information into corporate organizations controlled by financial groups, which were only interested in making large profits and did not care about the presentation of news. Taking into account the monopoly of news agencies and the growing costs of production and distribution, modern Marxists[11] argue that effective control over the means of information tends to be concentrated in the hands of a small number of capitalists whose ideas are thus widely disseminated and come to shape the minds of subordinate groups. According to this point of view the media, which are forced to rely increasingly on advertising revenue and external subsidies, and get their information from biased sources and which are vulnerable to the pressure of advertisers, bankers and politicians, play a crucial role in reproducing the power relations of capitalist societies. According to that view, ownership of the means of communication, economic power and class domination are closely connected and condition each other.

Before discussing Marxist theory, we must remember that the media have always developed under pressure of rising costs. Collecting news, selecting it and making it comprehensible for a wide range of non-specialist customers is very expensive. What is more, the technology which helps gather information, makes it available and transmits it does not stop changing. Minor 'revolutions' occurred with the development of optic telegraphy, the telephone, wireless telegraphy, teleprinters, satellites, fax and so on. Other important changes were brought about when stage coaches, then trains, then cars, then planes hastened distribution. Interestingly enough, the history of mass media, especially the history of the press has focused on a few individuals and on a limited range of 'revolutions' such as the so-called 'Northcliffe Revolution'. In fact contrary to what could be inferred from a sketchy historical account, new technical devices have been permanently introduced in the production of newspapers or broadcast programmes. Take the simple case of the recording equipment: it improves so fast that it has to be renewed every five years. In this field, innovation is ceaseless. How is it then possible to account for the selective, misleading version offered by many historians? By reference to the social cost of the successive, uninterrupted transformations which have affected the sector. Some innovations result in a staff increase. When the telephone became the best way of receiving instant news, most periodicals were obliged to recruit operators and stenographers. Or, to give another example, satellite news gathering, which began in 1980, allowed local stations to become independent of the big agencies; within a few years, tens of local and regional news bureaux flourished in the United States and recruited reporters. However, in other instances, technology has led to dramatic staff reductions. Such was the case when computerization was introduced in the processing of information during the 1970s. Journalists were first asked to key their reports directly into the computer, which reduced the numbers of printers employed. The crisis took a sharper form when computer terminals were used to assemble complete pages sent by satellite to printing plants miles away from the centre of production. Computerization resulted in a drastic cut in the workforce and provoked a violent, hopeless reaction by the unions. It was therefore called a 'revolution', and attention was focused on one point. This took away the attention paid to other previous or simultaneous changes.

Since they aim at maximizing their audience, or more simply, at avoiding any loss of clientele, most of the media are obliged to invest heavily. However, innovation, which plays a crucial economic role in the life of the major companies, is less important where local media are concerned. The main feature of the communal sector, referred to earlier, is that it draws its information from a limited, well-defined public, for example, a town, a society, a group of buffs. In this instance, consumers feel attached to their medium by a shared interest; they may even become informants as well as clients. Being aware of the fact that their paper or radio is their best, sometimes their only source of knowledge, they are used to asking questions and getting answers which help them face urgent, practical problems. Most of the time small magazines or broadcasting stations enjoy a monopoly in their sphere. Costs are kept down by voluntary or cheap labour and cheap production methods. Participation programmes invite listeners to call and join in discussions and printed sheets are distributed freely in shops. The technical quality is often inferior but the customers do not care since they are conscious that the work has been completed by non-professionals.

Local channels of information do not try to compete with the national media. However, far from living in a quiet, protected world, they are obliged to take into account the policy of the larger companies. In particular, they must be careful not to encroach upon advertising resources coveted by larger firms. What is more worrying is that, as soon as they become unable to stabilize their audience, they are under threat of absorption by conglomerates. This is precisely what happened in countries where broadcasting was deregulated during the 1970s. After an Italian court ruled that the state was not entitled to a monopoly of television advertisement, more than four thousand radio, and even television, stations were launched almost simultaneously. Most of them, lacking sufficient funding, soon became unviable and were bought up by a powerful commercial broadcasting group, Fininvest. Given the fact that they provided no profits and even generated losses, how can we account for Fininvest's decision? Answering the question is crucial for a correct understanding of the policy of the big networks.

News does not pay, but modern societies cannot develop without a permanent flow of fresh information. This is such a crucial necessity that governments have to integrate it into their policy. Public life in industrialized areas is dependent upon the distribution of news. As the information agencies face difficulties, some countries, for instance Sweden, have established a system of subsidies for the media. In other countries media mongers are released from charging VAT on newspaper sales or are offered free carriage. The state may also assume responsibility for transmitting the output of broadcasting stations. These are only partial, inadequate solutions. All the media enterprises, even when they are backed by the state, have to look to outside sources for extra finance and advertising remains the paymaster, in fact, the best way of providing reasonable income. Different media seek different publics. Some look for a general, ill-defined audience; others aim at targeted groups of consumers. Industrial companies which decide to set up a campaign for one of their productions do not want to waste time in finding the most suitable medium; they would prefer to deal with media companies likely to provide them with the most suitable group of consumers. Multi-media networks will therefore attract a volume of advertising superior to that offered to specialized networks. Let us return to the example of Fininvest. Since it encompasses Italy's most important advertising agency, it is an exception which is, however, likely to help us understand the strategy of smaller companies. Initially, the group was a publishing holding. In 1976 it set up a small television station in Lombardia. As Italian viewers were then tired of the unappealing programmes of the public networks, they welcomed the scheduling of American programmes, which were a great novelty. Advertising contracts began to blossom. The group improved its potential by forcing small stations to merge with Fininvest. It thus became a powerful commercial network and it combined with an advertising agency which enabled it to offer its clients a vast range of media and to secure a stable clientele.

The case of Fininvest is paradigmatic inasmuch as, in a short period of time, the conglomerate has succeeded in aggregating three publishing houses, a national newspaper and a few regional newspapers, a television network and an advertising agency. However, concentration is by no means a novelty; holdings have long existed in the realm of the media. The Victorian era saw the expansion of corporations where entrepreneurs developed their capital base by selling shares in their newspapers and the trend became more pronounced in the first decades of the present century. The Berry brothers, for instance, started with a magazine, *The Advertising World*, whose title was symptomatic. They progressed towards periodicals that specialized in food, health, pets and sport. Then, they took over the *Sunday Times*, the *Financial Times* and the *Daily Telegraph*, not to mention a series of provincial newspapers and a book publisher.[12] The Berrys confined themselves to managing newspapers but, in the 1930s, the American Henry Luce built up the first multi-media 'empire' by associating printed magazines and cinema. His *March of Time* was a monthly 20-minute released in about half of the American picture houses. It was not envisaged as an illustrated editorial but aimed to be a magazine deeply concerned with major contemporary issues. Conceived, in Luce's own terms, as 'fakery in allegiance to truth' it made the most serious problems look exciting by mixing up actual footage and scenes recreated by professional actors. Its stories were paralleled by those published in Luce's two weeklies, *Time* and *Life*. The magazines were twins but dealt with the same themes in a slightly different way. When the former, which was more political, stressed the dramatic or worrying aspects of a situation, the latter emphasized its emotional or sentimental side. In the same week *Time* would have a serious photograph on its cover and *Life* a pretty girl. Although personally a conservative, Luce was keen on keeping on his staff a few progressive journalists who would report on social problems such as poverty in rural areas or lack of medical care in the Deep South. As the Luce case makes it clear, diversification offers a way of limiting the losses on news gathering by creating a system of information exchange: the same data, collected by one group of staff, can be sold three times to three different media. Concentration also provides a chance to maximize the group's audience and therefore its appeal to advertisers.

However, in the world of information, diversification is not merely a necessary economic device. The possession of a wide range of media represents a considerable source of influence for the owner. It is not by chance that most of the press barons of the late nineteenth and early twentieth centuries had a seat in

Parliament, were knighted and were in constant contact with the other members of the ruling elite. One of them, Lord Rothermere, once observed that men like him 'come into newspapers as an ego trip'. After the Second World War the founding families were obliged to withdraw from their managerial role either because they were unable to cope with increasingly complex problems or because they had lost their majority of the shares. During the second half of the present century, important newspapers such as the *Daily Express*, the *Observer* and *The Times* have changed hands up to three times. Self-financing has become almost impossible; a series of bankruptcies has led to successive changes in ownership and new, larger conglomerates, including foreign interests have come onto the scene. This has often been depicted as the end of the era of press tycoons and the beginning of another era where share ownership is divorced from editorial management. The media, it is argued, have become mere pawns that conglomerates buy to revive them and then resell them when they are profit-making concerns – or, sometimes, when they have lost too much money. The *New York Post* was bought, in 1976, by Rupert Murdoch; having reorganized it, Murdoch sold the paper to buy a decaying television network; the new management was unable to maintain the tabloid; after six years it was on the verge of bankruptcy which allowed Murdoch to resume ownership at a favourable price. But Murdoch, however peculiar and purely speculative his strategy has always been, is still a media tycoon; his case shows that the era of the media barons is not over.[13]

More often than not media enterprises are merged into conglomerates, which have no experience in the production and distribution of information: the *Observer* was first rescued by an oil company, then by a conglomerate which was only marginally involved in the press business. As a rule, concentration is what occurs when a company with interests in one particular sector acquires interests in another sector. Acquisition, the argument goes on, does not imply a revolution in editorship; the group which gains control of a medium often keeps it as it was previously especially if it addresses a specific audience. When the *Daily Mirror* was absorbed by a conglomerate the new board did not change the staff of the paper, although its columnists were extremely critical of the establishment, because the *Daily Mirror*, by serving a largely working-class readership, reached a well-targeted consumer group. It could thus be defended that large concerns which tend to command leading positions in several sectors simultaneously and are mostly intent on making large profits, do not care about the content of the media. Modern enterprises involve regular activities distributed in a stable way and fulfilled continuously. These activities are entrusted to people who have gone through a prescribed course of training and are guaranteed a considerable wage: firing these people would be a strategic mistake. This view is usually called the 'managerial theory' because it assumes that in large corporations those who possess the necessary technical knowledge assume power in the organization.[14] Where media are concerned, the 'managerial theory' contends that editors and journalists, who are the only people able to gather, structure and distribute the news are themselves the managers.

Like any general statement, this is partially right, partially wrong. There have always been press barons intent on scrutinizing each issue of their papers and media moguls who do not want to interfere with the daily concerns of their staff. Good journalists are granted a high degree of autonomy but are never totally free. The crucial problem is to determine whether journalists' independence is limited by the control of the owners or by factors inherent in the very structure of media organizations. In its classical, restricted usage, the notion of organization refers to a social relationship which is closed, whose regulations are enforced by specific individuals and which is concerned with carrying into effect a given aim. In a television station, for instance, there is an authority and a staff which collects and broadcasts information. This is, at the same time, unquestionable and trivial. In his discussion of organizations[15] Weber provides what is missing in a purely functional analysis. He insists that the structure of an organization depends first, on the degree of specialization required for its different tasks (any medium has to inform, entertain, display adverts, etc.) and second, on the degree of stability guaranteed to the members. Both characteristics are in turn closely related to the development of production techniques and to the market situation. In other words, organizations must be placed in their social and economic context, they are dynamic, change-oriented parts of a global process.

We have already noted that making profits and acquiring fame are the two aims sought by most media moguls. These aims are not interconnected; they may even be contradictory, but few media owners can, or want to differentiate one from the other. They would rather believe that, eventually, money will supplement the social influence granted by the control of a medium. Why does a big Italian industrialist, Olivetti, who has built up an international empire in engineering and computers, buy a leading newspaper, *Repubblica*? Mostly because the paper has brought him additional prestige but also because it could bring some profit. Why does Bertelsmann, the giant German publisher, invest in records, films and audiovisual productions? Because it provides the group with a modern, younger image and because this is a way of expanding the profit potential of the distribution network. The ambitions of tycoons influence the transformation of the institutions that they rule. In buying or selling a paper or a network, capitalists participate in a general development of information which their personal concerns contribute to modify. This does not mean that sociology is obliged to question the motivation of moguls. Weber, who emphasizes purposive individual action, is careful to point out that the motives which guide people are simply a precondition of action. People's resolutions, Weber argues, are conditioned by their evaluation of opportunities and difficulties and by their perception of the available means. In the case of mass media the decisive factors that media owners have to evaluate are the state of the market, the evolution of techniques and the potential audience. Sociology must therefore concentrate on the interplay between individual aspirations and the socio-cultural whole in which information is manufactured and delivered.

Managing a medium implies urgent decisions and crucial choices. It is often said in newspaper offices that tycoons are preoccupied with hiring and firing but the pun misses the point. The running of a medium covers such difficult matters as the financing of losses, the acquisition of subsidaries, the definition of a commercial and editorial policy (for instance the transformation of the liberal, respectable *New York Post* into a sensationalist conservative tabloid), a transfer to a more convenient site (what happened when the *Manchester Guardian*, a provincial daily with a limited, regional circulation was turned into a national newspaper based in London). However complex they are, these questions could be dealt with by the editors and staff of a given medium. But there are other issues, namely those regarding technical changes and concentration which go much beyond the capacity of the executive personal. The media develop in capitalist, industrial societies where finance comes first and is itself conditioned by the progress of technology. While the executive personnel are preoccupied with *making* something (a paper, radio or television programmes), capitalists care about their relations with other companies. Financial and managerial links are crucial to the survival of any production company, however excellent its products are – and this is all the more true with media companies, whose productions are not always profitable. Any sociologist who takes the development of mass media as an object of study has to tackle the intricacies of financial and technological changes. We have noted, earlier, the part taken by the electricity industry in the launching of radio networks which helped it sell off its surplus stock: it was the capitalist market which transformed a military implement into a major means of communication. In a similar way record production and broadcasting have been closely linked right from their beginnings. Let us look at some implications of this relationship. A company like EMI which dominated the British record market during the second third of the twentieth century relied on radio to diffuse and consequently advertise its records. It soon had shares in RCA which involved it in research on television. The unexpected success of rock music, due to the cheap 45 LP that EMI did not produce allowed foreign companies such as Philips, for instance, to enter the British market, constraining EMI to offset losses in its record sector by investments in television. Decisions which influenced the development of broadcasting were determined partly by interlocking shareholdings which linked different corporations to each other and partly by rivalries or competition between the same sectors. Including a declining medium into a profitable conglomerate is a way of helping it survive. But the ties existing between the firms belonging to the conglomerate may lead to drastic change in the management of the medium.

Conflict between owners and managers are therefore unavoidable. The former decide on overall aim and define the means, scale and scope of production. The latter have to perform what has been settled over their heads and their independence is limited by the fact that they can be fired. This is not to say that editors and journalists are totally under control. As we shall see anon, the separation of ownership and daily administration is the rule in most media. Owners seldom intervene directly in the running of a newspaper or a broadcasting station. Disputes between them and the managers do not break out about content; they are provoked by decisions likely to modify the evolution of a medium as was the case, for instance, when computerization was introduced in the making of periodicals. In the late 1970s the financial problems that most dailies had to face demanded urgent solutions. It was necessary either to invest a growing volume of capital in production or to resort to computers which implied giving the sack to many printers. In the context of a capitalist society the managers could neither find the money nor consent to dismiss the workers. The owners were the only people who were in a position to choose, however damaging and arguable their choice was.

The distinction we have just made between management and effective power of decision is of paramount importance for an analysis of the media. It means that what matters for the owners is not what is 'said' but how their interests are furthered. This, in turn, limits the latitude given to the managers. These people can run a paper or a broadcasting station as long as a new economic orientation is not required. Economics come first, not because capitalists impose their ideas but because the life of any medium is conditioned by the evolution of industrial capitalism. It should then be realized why any model of communication, even when it embraces a wide range of functions and activities, is inadequate for a study of media. The inadaquacy stems from the fact that a medium is not only an intermediary between an emitter and an addressee but also a pawn in the strategy of its owner.

The problem of measuring the effects of tycoons' decisions upon the media market has been discussed earlier so that there is a need to draw a few putative conclusions from the debate. Even when they are intent on making money, media moguls aim more at expanding their domination than at making profits. Often, instead of getting rid of an unprofitable medium they place considerable emphasis on the past and on the reputation of this means of information. When a manufacturer cannot predict the benefit he will make in an extension of his firm, he will be cautious in developing it. The facts are otherwise in the media business. Even if the indicators of a claim for more information are not favourable, the media mongers do not miss any chance to expand their base. How is it possible to understand such seemingly nonsensical behaviour? What is at work is a different logic which goes beyond economic calculation. In the face of uncertainty the media monger is motivated by his fear that a rival could become stronger while the lack of relevant information about the future of a rather erratic market only tests his faith in the power of his expertise. What is encompassed in this is a recognition of the possibility of error and defeat in the process of assessing circumstances. Vulnerability has become a permanent characteristic of the press and broadcasting which have trouble preserving their economic stability. Corporate expansion, which is hardly a novelty and has been regularly developing since the Victorian era, helps meet liabilities. The influence of media owners and their capacity to overcome financial difficulties is reinforced through multiple directorships. But these schemes necessarily affect the evolution of the media.

PROFESSIONALS

In industrial societies three parameters are held to be of crucial importance to evaluate the productivity of an enterprise. The first is degree of professionalization, that is to say, the development and increasingly formalized transmission of specific skills under the control of experts. The second is the capacity of a firm to adapt its workers to their specific tasks and to reorientate them when the tasks change. The third is the dynamic relationship between the individuals and the organization that employs them. It is necessary to note that this evaluative framework, the validity of which is generally accepted, does not apply to the media.

A star system

An initial difficulty arises when we try to make an inventory of those who work in the media busness.[16] Take a case as simple as that of 'journalists'. They belong to unions[17] which can reveal how many of them there are. But only a limited portion of those who perform the function of a journalist join a union. The term covers people who spend all their working time gathering and disseminating news as well as part-time or occasional contributors who have activities more rewarding than their participation in the field. A politician, or a novelist who comment on current events once a month are journalists as well as a shopkeeper who collects local information, writes up notes and send them to a paper. Side aspects of the business namely photography, illustrating and script writing are also a useful additional source of income for experts but are rarely considered as permanent jobs. Independent work is exploited by the media since it is less expensive than professionalism. People working in an industrial or commercial branch have many things in common, the most conspicuous one being that they are interested in making a living. This is not at all the same in journalism. Money is not despised but its function is not as central as it is in other sectors. Voluntary or badly paid labour are exceptionally frequent in the media. For the pleasure of voicing their opinion people give their time freely or agree to a deferred-payment scheme whereby they will earn a percentage of the profits – should there ever be any. Some have come to the profession because it is a way of furthering an ideological commitment. Others are lured by the prospect of participating in important affairs and meeting great men or women. Of course, quite often, many different reasons overlap each other, making it difficult to explain the origin of a vocation.

Two-thirds of the people who work in media management are men. Among the women employees four-fifths are restricted to subordinate tasks with slim promotion prospects which implies that the most profitable jobs, editorship, journalism, reportage, are heavily male dominated. The basic training necessary to be recruited by a medium has never been clearly defined. There are a few excellent professional schools and universities that do degree courses in communication but the large majority of those involved in the field have been trained on the job. Students of journalism who are never mentioned in union statistics provide a good, inexpensive staff but the theoretical and practical skill they have gained does not secure them work and they can be easily supplanted by outsiders. At any rate, careers begin with long periods of work in the less prestigious sectors. Most people begin on weekly provincial newspapers, then spend some time on a local daily or a national periodical and end up, when they are lucky, on a national daily. The rate of turnover is particularly high in the media. This is a consequence of the ceaseless 'revolutions' which modify the distribution of jobs. For instance satellite news gathering which developed after 1980 challenged the long-established style of news bulletins so that, within a few years, all the big television networks had to make redundant about one-third of their information staff. Mobility is both a necessity for those who do not want to spend their entire life supplying local news to agencies and also a permanent threat; media people generally leave their job for better positions as soon as they can.

In terms of income, the differential between the diverse categories of employees is very substantial. In most businesses, variations in earnings are linked to the division of labour characteristic of capitalist enterprises. Industrial production involves a strict delineation of work to be done by manual workers, clerks, experts, executives and a hierarchical organization of many activities. The division of labour exists in the media, especially in television and cinema studios, but all the members of a filming team are professionals whose individual contribution is clearly specified and could not be left to unskilled workers. It must also be considered that the media generate little if any added value. All the wage earners, in the profession, live off the surplus value created in other sectors (mostly in sectors which pay, for instance, advertising). The multifarious categories contrived by media companies do not correspond to any defined skill. Who is able to distinguish a 'news director' from a 'news programme director', a news-reader from a newscaster? New, fanciful terms (anchor producer, anchorman) replace old ones (producer, announcer, introducer, presenter), styles change, from the perfect diction and graceful manners of the old BBC announcers to the witty, insolent, whimsical tone of anchor (wo)men introducing rock idols and sport stars, but all these people perform the same functions.[18] The routine tasks are demanding in both a local magazine and on a national television network. They require much competence and dogged persistence to ensure a reasonable standard of reliability from day to day. How is it, then, possible to account for the extensive range of salaries and promotion opportunities characteristic of the media? This is a seminal problem which has to be dealt with at length.

It is perfectly clear that both the moguls and their executives find it useful to leave the function of each member of their teams relatively imprecise. Vague, changing definitions allow the executives to control their staff better. The rate at which workers pass through the business is also a partial explanation. Even the stars or the most prestigious announcers are likely to be fired, which leads them to demand high salaries. However, this is an individual concern of stars and announcers, not a structural component of the media. If we want to explain the hierarchy of wages we must not stay inside the organizations. Stardom is a crucial aspect of the relationship between the media and the society in which they develop. The very existence of stars is vital for the media. Famous presenters are useful to market the products of their network whether these are films or broadcast programmes or magazines. But presenters serve broader ideological and economic ends first, by advertising various goods directly, second and more important, by representing specific values (how you should dress and behave to look fashionable) and affecting patterns of consumption. Radio and television presenters must create media events, advertise new conventions as potential revolutions and redesign the prevalent fashion by developing an intense interest in dressing, buying and travelling, according to the requirements of advertisers. Media stars are also important for the establishment. Being interviewed by a leading anchor (wo)man provides a politician, a sportsman or a musician with a label of potential fame. Magazines and broadcast programmes spend much space or time in measuring and confirming peoples' prestige. The range of possible solutions is widely extended. It begins with the star presenter introducing a personality-to-be and thus encouraging the audience to notice the newcomer. It goes on with chat shows in which the announcer and the guest lead an invited audience through a topical discussion and make it believe that they are both celebrities. There are also more up-market solutions, including programmes hosted by well-known people in which the interviewer looks happy to hear the memorable observations of the guest. Needless to say, interviews suit the media managers because they are cheap: guests appear for a nominal fee; the studio and the set are fixed, inexpensive costs. However, money is only one side of the business. The media and the establishment require one another for reciprocal advertisement. Star presenters are essential since they help gauge the status of their guests. Thousands of people carry out various tasks every day but they do not disclose themselves, they have to be revealed. This is something we have already stressed when studying the content of media: the world itself, including whatever might be counted as an 'event' has to be related; fame is not fixed, its definition changes according to the continuing evolution of societies. How is it possible to make a selection out of a wide range of sportspeople, singers, actors or politicians? Journalists tend to present their expertise as the answer to this puzzle. The determination of what deserves admiration is generally conventionalized but consumers do not usually notice this unless they are unaccustomed to the convention.

The influence of media stars is by no means a novelty, there were famous journalists in past centuries, journalists whose names were as famous as those of actors or generals. The wonder is that, if we compare the strategy and life work of such people, we can come to no conclusion. No rule explains why one becomes famous in this field. Some anchor (wo)men simply take advantage of existing audience predispositions aroused by previous programmes in order to provoke conditioned responses; in this case audiences applaud themselves and their own tastes and habits when they applaud the presenter. The accumulation of instantly recognizable details (clothes, the setting, etc., which are predictable and interchangeable), make it much easier for readers or viewers to feel at home with a journalist and endorse her or his opinion. Others make their reputation by discreteness; the trick is to present their guests or make comments in such a way that their language seems to speak for itself, simplicity and tact thus commanding sympathy. But the self-effacing are balanced by the self-regarding, those who have chosen to be snide, contemptuous or downright offensive and those who put questions in the form of propositions, forcing the interviewee either to agree or to look bad-tempered. Viewers or readers may conceivably imagine it is an easy task. In fact, the pressure on media stars is great; they do not stop working even under intense pressure and they are aware that their fame is transitory. Consider the idols of the past decade to see that they have been quickly forgotten.

The case of the media stars is rather challenging for any functional conception of societies. Functionalism tends to define possible connections between the importance of a social role and the competence of the agent who will perform it. However, no particular skill is required to be promoted to the rank of great presenter and no error or shortcoming explains why fame is so fleeting. It is also difficult to explain why demanding posts attract people who know perfectly well that they have no prospect of long-lasting success. If we want to make sense of that situation we must go beyond personal motivation and take into account the ideology of liberal societies. Liberalism is based upon a strong claim for equal treatment by citizens. Theoretically, people are granted the same prospects, all considerations of tradition or personal charisma have been abolished and individual capacity is the only criterion. What will mark out the most capable? Besides economics, which is the touchstone in a capitalist society, public fame is a seemingly unbiased, egalitarian yardstick. Fame may be gained in different ways but the media are surely the greatest makers and breakers of reputations. Now, the right to introduce the best singer or the best cricketer to the public is a form of power. Prestige, in the realm of the media, works at two different levels. Once a journalist has interviewed a statesman, other politicians want to be interviewed by the same person – the stature of the interviewee measures the social standing of the reporter and vice versa. The rewards are not negligible for presenters. Being a famous anchor (wo)man creates opportunities of developing personal contacts or alliances and to get recommendations and win a public reputation which may help find other jobs after having been sacked.

Between conflict and team spirit

The race for fame affects the life of media people both inside and outside their organization. At first sight the chances of becoming a columnist or the presenter of a popular programme seem to be equal. In his analysis of occupational groups Durkheim has stressed the significance of shared values, even in the context of rivalry. In most corporate bodies, the consciousness of belonging to a social entity is central in the self-esteem of all the members who abide by the established rules for the benefits they derive from them. In the case of media organizations where the team spirit is reinforced by the pursuit of important, socially valued aims, people are not merely content with providing good, accurate information, but also with using it to be given promotion.[19] It must not be forgotten, here, that the media may have a real influence on different sectors of a society and even on the power base. Let us take a simple example. In 1973 successive failure of the harvest in India left thirty-five million people facing severe hunger. The Indian government which was used to postponing practical decisions quickly, this time, instituted measures which prevented famine. The main reason why this occurred was that the Indian press campaigned for rapid relief. It is obvious that the authorities reacted because all necessary resources were at hand. The press campaign was merely a trigger. At any rate, the journalists could say that theirs had been a decisive intervention and those who had reported on the impending starvation had made a reputation for themselves. Courage, curiosity and cleverness, that is to say, individual qualities, seem all that is needed to be successful in the field. Inquisitiveness has long been the most highly praised quality of reporters because it is a way of implementing the policy of their employing organization and because it is the main road towards stardom.

Journalists give in to continuous network pressure; they are keen on recording history in the making, on getting as close to dramatic or exciting situations as possible and on giving their public accurate notions of what is going on in the world. They often claim that they are proud of a co-operative atmosphere based on creative work made together. It would not be hard to detect discrepancy between what is alleged and what is experienced. Competition worsens latent conflicts. For instance, it is not exceptional to see reporters appropriating the work of the photographer or cameraman who have investigated a story with them. Appearing centre stage, the journalists who provide a leader or a commentary insinuate that they have done alone what is the result of a collective effort. However, inasmuch as they assimilate the rules of their profession and adjust their strategy accordingly, most media people remain in line with Durkheim's analysis of professionals investments.

Professionals stress that media products must be subjected to certain norms. We shall look at these norms later when studying what the journalists tell their audience. First, we have to question the recurring claim for a better definition of individual roles for this seems to imply that responsibilities are not clearly specified. Those collaborating in media production contend that they experience their life as torn between contradictory goals. They work, it is argued, according to their perception of audience requirements but, in doing so, they often miss the demands of the organization. Up to now we have explained how journalists or presenters attempt to show that they are the best at their job because the world of media is dominated by the law of competition. But factors other than reaching a wider audience interfere in the management of a medium. The overlapping of different tasks, both economic and non-economic, is a source of persistent tension. While speaking of the team and its life we have lost sight of its direction. We now need to scrutinize the relationship between the executives and the media professionals.

Media owners, together with the board of directors, fix the scale and scope of production and decide on overall aims. Then they relinquish their control over current operations and leave the routine management to full-time executives. As a rule, media managers should have considerable autonomy at the practical level. However, theirs is a rather awkward situation. They occupy positions of formal authority and have the difficult task to adapt to the strategy of the owners while coordinating the activities of those who write the papers or make the programmes. They are generally intent on improving the quality of their product. But they know that the media have always obtained more money from advertising than from their public and, for that reason, they attempt to maximize the space available for adverts. At the same time, their budget has to be strictly controlled; they are not the men who buy information and pay editors, it is their job to save money and to prevent their reporters or photographers from spending too much.

In a context of permanent competition, any medium must maintain its audience and try to augment it. The number of potential clients is not indefinitely extensible; it is a narrow band of indecisive customers constantly wavering from a medium to another. Those clients are people who have ill-defined opinions. Conformity is therefore the best way of seducing them. We have already noted a blatant lack of originality and imagination in many papers and broadcast programmes. The blame lies partly with the sources of information. There are only five news agencies and, since news gathering is expensive, many media derive the bulk of what they will announce from a single agency. As well as news agencies we have identified another major source of information – the official services, especially the police. Given the origins of most material, it is not surprising that media offer a sizeable sample of conventional wisdom. Executives find it crucial to minimize the risk of offending or irritating any putative section of the public. Media executives have sometimes been called 'professional populars' which means that they care about public taste and tend to tell the news in the way in which the average customer is accustomed to getting it. When journalists or playwrights bring them proposals, the executives merely decide whether it is likely to appeal to the public. Experience has told them that some images or, less commonly, some sentences endure as established forms of depicting welfare or poverty, love or hatred, hope or despair and have to recur again and again whenever these topics are mentioned. For instance, documentaries and written reports have traditionally used images of the tramp, of the disaffected and alienated veteran, of the immigrant unable to adjust to another, more advanced society. These formulas have been endlessly re-employed in the journalistic, cinematic and televisual depiction of vagrants wandering through suburban streets, veterans returning from various wars, aliens ready to steal and kill, in spite of the dissimilar situations in which unemployment, war or immigration took place. The executives are inclined to maintain well-tried and tested formats. They resist change and favour routine programmes to which audiences have been long accustomed. They allege that repetition does not necessarily mean bad quality and boredom but may be an incitement to explore the complexities of seemingly 'frozen' genres.

This is what makes the media professionals feel uneasy. Market considerations, they say, force them to use common-place rather than original expressions. At the same time higher wages and promotion depend on their ability to do a good, innovative job and they are permanently prompted to compete with one another. In business, advancement is generally closely linked to output – better results entail more money available for the staff. However, quantity is not a gauge for the media since their owners strive simultaneously towards different goals, seeking, as has been argued earlier, both fame and money. Working for a medium is not therefore like working for any industrial firm. If the job implies ambition, the daily routine far from being exciting, soon becomes rather humdrum. It is in this context that team spirit has to be evaluated. The notion of some sort of organizational identity helps balance frustrated personal aspirations and resists managerial control. It can be seen as a kind of moral engagement that will last through time. Imaginary though it is, the pact turns out to be effective. But those who work in the media are not only (and not mostly) paid to maintain the organization. What they have to do is to inform the public. The organization (a newspaper, a broadcasting station) provides a place within which it is possible to elaborate on news. But the moguls do not aim at disseminating news; they sell news to fulfil other purposes. This leads us to deal with a major ambiguity of the media: who will define what should be told?

Telling what?

Objectivity, or rather, honesty, is the most prized among qualities required from journalists. However, explaining what 'objectivity' means is impossible. Journalists belong to a culture, the prejudices and values of which they share. During the war in the Transvaal, Emerson Neilly told in the *Pall Mall Gazette* how adolescents who were defending a Boer trench had been bayoneted by British soldiers. While admitting that this had been a dirty job he could not help adding that 'if any shame attaches to the killing of the youngsters it must rest on the shoulders of those fathers who brought them there'.[20] Stubborn patriotism? Or the mere incapacity to think outside the logic of one's country's unquestionable rectitude? Investigators do not stay on the sidelines; they are direct witnesses of dramatic situations; their objectivity is necessarily impaired by the impossibility to remain aloof. Aloysius MacGahan, commissioned to report on the atrocities of Turkish forces against the Christians in Bulgaria, wrote in the *London Daily News*, on 26 July 1876, 'I came in a fair and impartial frame of mind. I fear I am no longer impartial and I am certainly no longer cool. There are things too horrible to allow anything like calm inquiry'.[21]

Honesty might be nothing more than a resolute avoidance of any conscious lie. It is surely deceitful to film natives who have learned to earn money by performing their dances to visiting cameramen and then to contend that the resulting documentary pictures rituals which might be lost soon. It is indecent to fake an interview by interposing fake questions among statements made by a personality that (s)he is said to have answered. It is unfair to substitute a person's speech with a voiceover instead of giving them a chance to speak for themselves. All these examples are blatant cases of fraud. However, although such things have occurred, they do not deserve to be discussed at length. But things are seldom as simple as that. Many factors are likely to obscure a reporter's critical view. News-gatherers are generally asked to bring back information as soon as possible. Their first sources are the news agencies and the other media (for instance, the broadcast media for the newspapers) which means that what they get from the start is data that has already been selected and written up. Experienced reporters have personal contacts whom they call or visit. Since the informants often want, or are obliged, to remain anonymous it is tempting to quote them directly, without acknowledging the possible bias of the source. It is at any rate extremely difficult for journalists to depart from the point of view of their usual correspondents. For instance, a news-gatherer who depends on the police for information will not be quick to question allegations made by the police. This does not imply any collusion, it is a question of common sense: the institutions which disseminate information have more trust in the people they know; conversely, specialist journalists have a better understanding of the institutions which they visit frequently.

Every morning a multitude of news stories are released to editorial offices. How is it decided that an item of news must be passed on to the public? Editors usually give a twofold answer.

There is, they argue, on the one hand, the information likely to serve people in their day's business (from the weather forecast to the foreign exchange rates) and, on the other, widely publicized information that is part of the common awareness of what is going on in the world. However simple and acceptable it is, the distinction does not help to clarify practical issues. Let us move from considering generalities to more concrete matters. In Denmark, in 1993, a male prostitute who knew that he was infected, and persisted in having intercourse with men and women, was charged for deliberately spreading AIDS. As he had had many sexual partners a tabloid newspaper, *Extrabladet*, printed a full-page photograph of the man on the front page, it was said, to inform the victims. In that instance informing the public is clearly a poor excuse for abject sensationalism. But the dividing line between what is fair and what is not is seldom that obvious. Is it unfair to tell the inhabitants of a town that a banker or a shopkeeper are being sued for cheating on their customers? We are not concerned here with solving the problem. What matters is that, at any rate, a choice has to be made and that it is, to a large extent, a subjective one.

The fact that news is produced by news-gatherers and that it is not a pure reflection of facts, has become a well-established approach amongst sociologists. But this does not boil down to a mere question of selection. What is told in the media has to be carefully presented. Agencies or private informants communicate data, i.e. crude data. After taking a glance at the news Virginia Woolf once said that, in too many periodicals, 'life itself escapes'. If they want to bring 'reality' to their newspapers journalists have to concern themselves not with the externals of what is happening but with 'life' as it is perceived and experienced by people. Their task is to engage viewers or readers in the account of how other human beings confront different, sometimes dramatic situations. By doing this, they cannot avoid mixing facts with opinions, explanations and a touch of emotion. When writing or speaking in a lively, accessible style journalists often resemble novelists, style being more important than the facts themselves. However objective an announcer claims to be, there is always a note of friction in a news bulletin and rhetoric plays its part in making a piece of information relevant. Here we enter a no-man's land between truth and bluff. What happens when details are missing or when witnesses are reluctant to speak? A well-known very effective, dirty trick is for a reporter to adopt a false identity whilst employing covert photography. But journalists do not need to go that far to be on the verge of lying. In 1938, at a time when television was still in its infancy, a German professional, Friedrich Gladenbeck, imagined what could be done to make spectators 'take part' in an event. He envisaged that the German troops had conquered a city:

> An announcer could first point out the line of advancement on a map, and then mix in some pictures of the city from our archives, and then show the most current footage we have of the marching troops, etc. Through the skilled use of the means available to us, the viewer would get the impression of live coverage even from the broadcasting of still photographs.

Early cinematographers had anticipated Gladenback by filming the Spanish–American War of 1898 with scale models of ships in a pond. In fact, forgery has been used for centuries in reporting wars, disasters and floods, etc. Imagine that a paper which is trying to comment on a car crash and which has no photograph of the accident, decides to print, instead, a picture of another, similar crash: it does not fake the event and the picture is not a fraud. However the connection of these items is dishonest. Again, starting from very simple, ordinary situations (calling the police, questioning a witness) we have come, little by little, to the crudest falsification.

What is disturbing about Gladenback's statement is that he is in no doubt about the legitimacy of his fraud. The reporter or the team who have investigated an event are eager to report its distinctive features. They are prompted by a sincere desire to do good work and please their public. A nice framing and an interesting background are likely to promote the power of a story filmed in that context. Celluloid glamour which captivates audiences is also welcomed by the producers who believe that it will make the finished product more exciting. But this requires adaptation not of film to facts but of facts to film. James Francis Hurley, one of the few cameramen who covered both world wars, used to say that he was seeking 'spectacular results', which implied the making of 'dramatic pictures carefully planned, finely composed and subsequently promoted with skill'. Hurley was not a fraud, he took considerable risks to photograph what was happening on the front line and his photographs were genuine. Yet, was he filming 'objective' or 'spectacular' situations? Photographers and editors will argue that people do not look at a poor picture, whereas they learn something from excellent photography.

The business of informing the public carries inherent contradictions: between speaking factually and providing illuminating comments; between leaving the public in a state of uncertainty and lulling it into a comfortable certitude. Media makers know that the crucial facts, the ones which would allow them to fully account for a situation often remain inaccessible and that they have to sort things out for themselves. Necessary though they are, the duties of an impartial chronicler do not usefully have a bearing on the actual task of delivering understandable news to audiences. In the realm of media, scepticism concerning objectivity paradoxically becomes confused with the belief in the essential function of the media. Unsatisfactory though it is, the effort to collect as many facts as possible and to relate them in a wider context is perceived as a social obligation. This is something that must be borne in mind when trying to make a sociological analysis of media workers. Journalism is an occupational category. As such, it is characterized by its recruitment, its economic reward, its role and its tenets. As has been said, media professionals are drawn from diverse backgrounds with no marked-out, compulsory curriculum and no marketable technical knowledge is required from them. Journalists rank high on the salary scale but there are tremendous differences in their wages which results in harsh competition and thrusting individual ambition. These characteristics which entail a low level of co-operation are balanced by two other features. Since media people work for owners and executives who have little interest about news content, it is up to them to define their tasks and to establish ethical rules governing their work. Theirs is a symbolic skill which they protect and enhance systematically and which provides them with a relatively high degree of integration. Like the majority of professionals, journalists have no control over their means of production. But, unlike other salaried employees they are not alienated from the product of their labour. They are therefore keen to protect their independence and they consider it to be their responsibility to decide what news can or cannot be disseminated. However, their relative freedom does not sanction any specific mission, it is the result of the dual structure of media organizations.

Economically the media are partly typical of but partly quite different from capitalist enterprises. They are similar in that they are strongly influenced by technical changes, they necessitate huge investment and they are included in conglomerates. They differ, however in being not primarily profit oriented and in seeking several aims simultaneously. Given the role of property in capitalism, the media moguls also retain effective power. They could sell their companies exclusively to make money but that would result in high prices and a limited circulation. In this instance, their power would be limited to the management of one medium. Besides institutional authority, free societies exhibit various forms of domination whereby influential people are able to realize their ambitions over and above the will of the majority. Ascendancy cannot be measured; in some cases it is a capacity to manipulate political decisions, in others it is moral leadership. Aspiring to domination is chancy. The control of a medium is said to bring some prestige, leadership candidates become media owners while media moguls believe that they may influence events; hence, the strategies of media organizations, the constitution of networks and the ambiguous, fragile independence granted to the professionals.

NOTES

1 The Independent Television Act of 1954 created a private, commercial sector of television, ITV, Independent Television, began to broadcast in 1955.
2 The early and mid-1920s were a period of serious unrest in Europe. The British strike of 1926, the first to be reported by radio, was denounced by conservative politicians and newspapers as a prerevolutionary event.
3 The BBC, such as it was set up by the 1926 Charter, is not a governmental body. However, it is under government control, it gets its money from the Treasury, its governors are appointed by the government. It is independent inasmuch as it remains clear of direct political affiliation but its independence is the best way of avoiding any intervention of the government.
4 M. Pegg, *Broadcasting and Society, 1918–1939* (1983, London, Croom Helm).
5 The Act regulated the granting of frequencies. Taking advantage of this regulation the big networks could suppress most independent stations.
6 In the same way, in Nazi Germany, television was conceived

as a medium for collective viewing; home consumption was drastically limited and television halls where up to 400 people could gather were built in Berlin and diffused news bulletins up to the end of the war.

7 M. Weber, *Economy and Society*, (1978, Berkeley, Los Angeles and London, University of California Press), p. 212; see also p. 53ff and p. 941ff. It must be noted that Weber who gives many examples of domination (banking, food or coal and oil supply), never mentions the case of the press.

8 J. C. Robertson, *The Hidden Camera: British Film Censorship in Action 1913–1972* (1989, London, Routledge).

9 On the relationship between newsreel companies and the British government, see A. Aldgate, *Cinema and History. British Newsreels and the Spanish Civil War* (1979, London, Scolar Press) p. 77ff.

10 On Reuters and on the financial side of news agencies see D. Read, *The Power of News. The History of Reuters, 1819–1989* (1992, Oxford University Press) especially p. 295ff.

11 See especially N. Chomsky and E. S. Herman, *Manufacturing Consent. The Political Economy of Mass Media* (1988, New York, Pantheon Books). It must be noted that this book is a lampoon based on little factual evidence. It is interesting inasmuch as it provides a systematic development of Marx's thesis.

12 On the Berry family, see D. Hart-Davis, *The House the Berrys Built. Inside the Telegraph, 1928–1986* (1989, London, Hodder). A general survey of the British press is provided by C. Wintour, *The Rise and Fall of Fleet Street* (1991, London, Century Hutchinson).

13 It is not my aim, in this book, to examine the strategies of tycoons. Excellent, up-to-date information is to be found in J. Tunstall and M. Palmer, *Media Moguls* (1991, London, Routledge).

14 In its most sophisticated version the theory is exposed by R. Dahrendorf, *Class and Class Conflict in an Industrial Society* (1959, London, Routledge & Kegan Paul) p. 46ff.

15 See note 7, *Economy and Society*, p. 48ff.

16 S. R. Lichter, S. Rothman and L. S. Lichter, *The Media Elite* (1987, New York, Adler and Adler).

17 For Britain, statistics are given by the National Union of Journalists and by the Institute of Journalism but the figures do not reveal more than the number of people who have joined a union.

18 'Announcer' was coined as soon as broadcasting began, in 1923 the term was in current usage in the *Radio Times*. 'Introducer' and 'presenter' came into use two decades later. 'Anchorman' surfaced after the Second World War in the USA where it was used during the 1948 presidential campaign. It reached Britain in the middle of the 1960s.

19 D. C. Hallin, *We Keep America on Top of the World. Journalism and the Public Sphere* (1993, London, Routledge) analyses the work of journalists and shows how theirs is simultaneously a profit-making, rewarding and politically influent job.

20 P. Knightely, *The First Casualty* (1976, New York, London, HBJ), pp. 57–58.

21 Knightely, p. 50.

Conclusion

Mankind is a species seeking meaning. Human beings try to make sense out of their daily experience, and to understand the situations they have to face and would like to anticipate what might result from these situations. The fact that, quite often, explanations turn out to be inadequate does not prevent people from making connections and using them to throw light on the present and the future. Information is crucial in this respect for it makes people see the circumstances in a different light: the more we know, the more we believe that we can provide new, complex explanations. Information has long been the fabric of 'facts' in terms of which human beings interpret their lives and guide their actions.

Sometime between the sixteenth and the eighteenth centuries there were, in the Atlantic world, dramatic socio-technological changes. Trade and industrialization developed simultaneously thus empowering western communities to develop on both a physical and an intellectual plane. Thanks to the advent of modern methods of communication, information followed the general trend. It would be meaningless to ask whether the cause was an increase in supply or a rise in demand: both overlapped and influenced each other. A vast expansion in the range of goods available was accompanied by a desire to know more about what was happening beyond the small circle in which people used to live. Clearly, this was linked to the needs of trade and curiosity was intensified by the increasing availability of information. Today, we are still involved in an ongoing process which began before we were born and will go on for a good many years. Historians have rightly stressed the most significant changes (the so-called 'revolutions') which have marked the evolution of the means of conveying information for a number of centuries but, as soon as we ignore chronology, we cannot help but notice an impressive continuity. The case for taking a long view of this evolution is a powerful one which has important implications about how the development of dissemination of news is understood. Taking a long perspective, interest in information is likely to appear less as a passing fancy and more as an integral part of industrialization. In this respect the most modern means of conveying information cannot be assigned to the exclusive influence of financial conglomerates and the latest advances in technology. The development of the press and broadcasting has not simply been a matter of knowing more about the world, it has been an aspect of a move from one kind of society to a profoundly different one. Paraphrasing Raymond Williams[1] we could say that today the supply of news has become as necessary as the supply of food or fuel and that this supply is met and its distribution organized in much the same way. Mankind has become eager for information and as consumers are longing for news, news has been transformed into a good, i.e. something that can be bought and sold. The massive consumption of information is akin, at least in the industrial world, to the massive purchase of material goods and the mechanical reading or viewing (for instance, channel-hopping) are not unrelated to the mechanical habits of work.

The various methods for the dissemination of information have been grouped together in a catch-all term, 'mass media', which encompasses a greatly diverse variety of technical devices and communication practices into a single, critically manageable whole. The word 'mass' seems to imply that quantity makes the difference. Considering the viewpoint of a slow, long-lasting evolution which has been defended in this book, it is a rather misleading term. The first newspapers had a limited circulation but they were already participating in the protracted change which had been voiced earlier. The emergence of the printed press and of the advertisements it was immediately designed to carry was the beginning of a new historical period, even if the mass of people did not handle a paper for at least two centuries. The term 'medium' is more relevant provided it is taken in its original sense, namely something by or through which two distant points are put in touch. It has been constantly argued in this book that the means of communication generate a twofold movement and that the addressees are also emitters. In this respect a newspaper or a broadcast programme are 'media'.

The expression 'mass media' has become accepted through use; we cannot avoid it but we must be aware of its inadequacy. It calls to mind an idea of coherence and oneness whereas the world of information has never been a unitary, fixed whole but a decentred, fragmentary assemblage of conflicting voices and institutions; a plurality of separate practices in competition with each other for audience. Various strands of social life have come together, for about four centuries, and have created the present situation in which people, throughout the world, are overwhelmed by news, adverts and audiovisual texts. Yet, the notion of a kind of entity, 'the media', which might be connected by the fact that they sell the same materials, namely news, is no longer sufficient. We have to face a paradoxical situation. One evolutionary pathway can be traced from the seventeenth century to the present day: there is a close relationship between the development of information and the growth of audiences. However, there is also a gap between the first, handprinted papers and the sophistication of virtual, computerized images. Today all the media have recourse to the same sources and talk about the same data. But these media are founded on different practices – some exist as a result of voluntary work, whilst others are linked to the economy of scale, standardization and vertical integration and the former as well as the latter are threatened by their own technological evolution. Indeterminacy is chronicled in the evolution of the media and results in sudden, unpredictable changes.

The difficulties inherent in any general definition of the media has often been blurred because, since the eighteenth century, theoreticians have been mostly interested in the problem of opinion and opinion-making. For those who believe that opinion can be formed or shaped, it is very much a part of the question of power. There has been an enduring attempt to understand the relationship between the production of information, such as can be found in the newspapers or, later, in broadcast programmes, and perceived or subjective news, i.e. news as it is received and interpreted by the public. What we term as 'modernism', which was the inheritance of the Enlightenment, was obsessed with the quest for clear explanations. It wanted to clarify what media were made for, it emphasized their ideological power, their capacity to persuade. Marxism, the most sophisticated attempt at explaining the ideological power of the means of disseminating information, was extremely useful in showing how capitalism tends to control public opinion and camouflages it behind its proclaimed interest for truth. What it explained about the relationship between money and the mass media, about the economic determination of information still seems valid. But this does not mean that economically determined media produce ideology in order to enslave the workers and keep them in their position of domination. The self-transformation of economic systems can be achieved without recourse to propaganda; capitalism, in its present stage, does not need to mobilize legitimation or to enforce habits of consumption. To a large extent, the 'content' of media is granted unprecedented freedom of development because what is said or shown does not matter. It is always possible (though not necessarily likely) for people to rearrange the patterns disseminated by the media. Marxism is flawed by stressing a monolithic, dominant vision of the world rather than a cacophony of conflicting ambitions employing diverse strategies of legitimation.

This book is based on the conviction that there is no general theory likely to account for the nature and functions of the media but instead, a range of relationships and connections that can be invoked when it is necessary to explain a particular situation. It is also a critical essay aimed at recalling that we are all media consumers and at questioning the readers about their practice of obtaining information. A major task of sociology is to explore human bonding. How do individuals participate (or refuse to participate) in groups which condition their own experience and which are constructed by them? The cohesion of human groups is achieved through various institutions, some of which are the media. It is common sense to start on safe ground by scrutinizing what people buy, and how much time they spend watching television or reading a paper. These studies may illuminate particular aspects of the question but it would be misleading to go on collecting evidence in the hope of improving our awareness of the role played by the media in modern societies. What we can infer from the observation of daily life is highly hypothetical; it is what we could call, after David Chaney, 'a statistical fiction': given the pre-eminence of certain themes in the media, we tend to believe that the readers/viewers may have noticed them. But we shall forever be ignorant of how each individual has received what they have been told and how the interaction of various individuals has created an interpretation of the news. We have therefore tried to go beyond the classic, satisfactory but in the end oversimplified vision of media as the means of 'telling' us something. This is not to say that media are totally vacuous or are governed by fantasy but that we cannot be satisfied with analysing their 'messages'.

We have therefore begun by looking at some of the relationships which develop between different social formations and the media. Newspapers and then radio have long provided a pretext or an occasion around which various groups could gather in common activities. The circulation of news has created links between individuals, thus creating sociations which have in turn sent back information to other sociations. We have come to no conclusion. Questions and uncertainties remain. How do people choose their sources of information? Do they tend to use information collectively or individually? How are their practices affected by age, gender, social status, profession, political beliefs? What is to be learned from literary criticism, from publicity, from sales or from the letters individuals send to professionals (e.g. letters to the editor in newspapers)? The variety of possible perspectives is a real challenge but our purpose in this work is not to centre on any single issue, it is to stimulate the sociological imagination of the readers.

Mass media provide the illusion of immediacy of the world around us. However, we are all well aware of the discrepancy that exists between what goes on, day after day, around us, and what is reported; we know that words and even a photograph can distort reality. The media testify to the world that they have an investigative role but they are not impassive witnesses; their presentation of facts is biased by changing intellectual, social and cultural assumptions. Without the media we would ignore what is happening beyond our immediate surroundings but they force us to perceive things via their unspoken prejudices. Gross misrepresentations have often provoked hostile reactions against the sensationalism of the popular press and television. Sociologists have a right to condemn what they find inadmissible but theirs is not an ethical vocation; they are not entrusted with evaluating the role played by the media in the evolution of public morality. Political and social activities in a liberal society, where instructions do not come from above, cannot be sustained without permanent exchange of services and goods – news being one good among many others. Making use of a medium dominates our leisure time today and it is thanks to the media that we have knowledge of the outside. What matters, then, is not what has been said in this medium on that topic, but the all-pervasive omnipresence of the media in our lives. Advertisements exemplify in immediately perceptible forms the variety of the media market. Adverts simultaneously address different audiences, thus making diversity a deliberate means of defining communities of the same inclination and diffuse messages that are comprehensible to virtually everybody. There is an intriguing contrast between the flexibility, the ill-defined character of what is chronicled in the media and the increasing number of media addicts. Our ancestors interpreted the world by obeying the word of god or a king. Today we interpret the world through magazines or television. This is one of the main issues in this book at least where what is said (i.e. the 'contents') is concerned. It is not the sociologist's job to decide to what extent the images conveyed in the media are faithful to reality (this would be a metaphysical question implying an indisputable definition of reality), but how the actual, physical universe is involved in media productions. Reporters and journalists observe some portions of the outside world and insert them in concrete, material objects such as magazines, cassettes and records which are sold and bought and produce financial 'realities'. All newspapers or broadcast programmes offer to the public partial, therefore fictional universes, which have their own internal coherence, which are accepted by the public and which help individuals to make sense of reality.

News is sold on a mass market. Since their origin the media have adapted to the volume of trade and at the same time they have made a major contribution to its enlargement and modification. Their strategy has had many parallels with the development of industrial manufacturing. Like factories the various sectors of news production have always been intent on finding more buyers and their simultaneous evolution has led them to create huge networks. Concentration and internationalization have characterized the media as well as most other industries.

However, the world of the media is singular inasmuch as, unlike other industries, its primarily aim is not making money. The ownership as well as the production of any medium brings fame. In societies where power is not stable but is continually renegotiated between competing groups the control of a medium is an invaluable source of influence. As a 'product' any media item is conditioned by the evolution of technology, the degree of standardization and the increase in demand. But those who own it and use it to strengthen their social domination are less concerned with money than with reputation; they are keen to separate possession from management and sometimes to face heavy losses.

The assumptions defended in this book and summarized in this concluding section should have made clear the reasons why it is difficult, if not impossible, to offer any general theory about the complexity involved in the creation and development of the media. This is why we have claimed from the outset, our debt to the theory of deconstructionism, a worrying but exciting approach which challenges any systematic analysis of social phenomena. In the three spheres that we have researched – audiences, the content of the media and the media makers – we have noted that simultaneously, they provoke change, are the channels through which changes happen in other sectors and are conditioned by the evolution of the society. This may sound disappointing but readers must not forget that sociology is first and foremost concerned with delimiting problems and elaborating the concepts likely to help make order from the available data. In other words, for a sociologist, asking the right questions is more important than transient answers.

NOTES

1 R. Williams *Reading and Criticism* (1950, London, Frederick Muller), p. 9.

Suggestions for further reading

The aim of this book is not to examine the media as static entities but rather to understand them as an inexplicable process without reference to the general system in which they are merged. For that reason little has been said about the different methods of communication. The suggestions made in the following bibliography supplement the references contained in the notes at the end of each chapter and may help the reader find the relevant sources concerning each medium.

NEW TRENDS IN COMMUNICATION STUDIES

Ben, A., *The Decline of Discourse. Reading, Writing and Resistance in Postmodern Capitalism* (1990, New York, The Falmer Press.)

Collins, R., ed., *Media, Culture & Society* (1986, London, Sage).

Edelman, M. J., *Constructing the Political Spectacle* (1989, University of Chicago Press).

Ferguson, M., ed., *Public Communication: the New Imperatives. Future Directions for Media Research* (1990, London, Sage).

Kearney, R., *The Wake of Imagination: Toward a Postmodern Culture* (1988, Minneapolis University Press).

McQuail, D., *Mass Communication Theory: an Introduction* (1987, London, Sage).

ECONOMIC AND SOCIAL CONTEXT OF MEDIA DEVELOPMENT

Brewer, J. and Porter, R. eds, *Consumption and the World of Goods* (1992, London, Routledge).

Coarse, R. H., *The Firm, the Market and the Law* (1988, University of Chicago Press).

Curran, J., *Media, Power and Politics* (1993, London, Routledge).

Golding, P. ed., *Communicating Politics* (1986, Leicester University Press).

Inglis, F., *Media Theory: an Introduction* (1990, Oxford, Blackwell).

Katz, E. and Szecsko, T. eds., *Mass Media and Social Change* (1981, London, Sage).

Marvin, C., *When Old Technologies were New: Thinking about Electric Communication in the Late Nineteenth Century* (1989, New York, Oxford University Press).

Strasser, S., *Satisfaction Guaranteed. The Making of the American Mass Market* (1989, New York, Pantheon).

MONOGRAPHS

Antonelli, C. ed., *New Information, Technology and Industrial Change: the Italian Case* (1988, Boston, Dordrecht, London, Kluver Ac. Publishers).

Barnow, E., *A History of Broadcasting in the United States. I. – A Tower in Babel; – II. – The Golden Web; – III – The Image Empire* (1966–1970, New York, Oxford University Press).

Corry, J., *Television News and the Dominant Culture* (1986, Washington, Media Institute).

Curran, J. and Seaton, J., *Power without Responsibility: the Press and Broadcasting in Britain* (1985, London, Methuen).

Domahue, H. C., *The Battle to Control Broadcast News* (1989, Cambridge Mass., MIT Press).

Drummond, P. and Peterson, R. ed., *Television in Transition* (1985, London, BFI).

Gomery, D., *Shared Pleasures: A History of Movie Presentation in the United States* (1992, University of Wisconsin Press).

Hetherington, A., *News, Newspapers and Television* (1985, London, Macmillan).

Kellner, D., *Television and the Crisis of Democracy* (1990, Oxford, West View Press).

Kubey, R. W. and Csikszentmihalyi, J., *Television and the Quality of Life: How Viewing Shapes Everyday Experience* (1990, Hillsdale, N.J. Erlbaum).

Livingstone, S., *Making Sense of Television* (1990, London, Pergamon Press).

McNair, B., *News and Journalism in the UK* (1993, London, Routledge).

Sterling, C. H. and Kittross, J. M., *Stay Tuned: A Concise History of American Broadcasting* (1990, Belmont, CA, Wadsworth).

Wallis, R. and Baran, S., *The Known World of Broadcast News. International News and the Electronic Media* (1990, London, Routledge).

Williams, R. *Television, Technology and Cultural Form* (1974, London, Fontana).

Index